Jihad b

To Strive by Means of the Pen

Tri-City Action for Peace

Edited by
Marc Beaudin

Heal the Earth Press

First Edition.

Published by Heal the Earth Press; Saginaw, Michigan. Printed by InstantPublisher.com. For ordering information and other Heal the Earth publications, visit: http://healtheearth.tripod.com (no "www").

For information on Tri-City Action for Peace, visit: www.tcap.mahost.org.

Cover art by Jason Graham. Design by Marc Beaudin.

ISBN: 1-59196-708-2

Acknowledgments

Thanks to all the members of TCAP, especially Mark and Jo Kraych; to Jason Graham for his art and fundraiser coordinating, to Lisa Purchase Gould for proofreading and invaluable editing suggestions; to the artists who donated artwork to our auction: Chad Adamowski, Steve Barber, Collective Artists' Gallery & Exchange (CAGE), Jason Graham, Robert Graham, Kellie Schneider, and Tim Speaker, as well as the Red Eye Coffeehouse for hosting it; to the bands who performed at our fundraising concert: Astra, Matt Besey & Caitlin Berry, Continental Blue, Al Hellus & the Plastic Haiku Band, The Mongrels, The Saginaw Jazz Quartet, and Stamp'D, as well as the Hamilton St. Pub for hosting it; to everyone who supported our fundraising events, gave donations, and pre-ordered copies to make publication possible; to everyone who submitted their work to create this book; and finally, to everyone everywhere who works to find peaceful solutions to our conflicts, build non-violent communities, and struggle against all odds for truth and justice.

Tri-City Action for Peace
Mission Statement

Tri-City Action for Peace works for global peace and justice through nonviolent resistance. To this end, we will:

1) build a community which lives and celebrates nonviolence and peace;

2) raise awareness of the consequences of violence, in domestic issues and foreign policy; and

3) create opportunities for people diverse in beliefs and cultures to participate in nonviolent resistance and protest against all forms of violence.

For more information or to join TCAP, please visit

www.tcap.mahost.org.

Striving by Means of the Pen -
A Work in Progress

Seeing the word "*Jihad*" on the cover of an anti-war book may seem at first a contradiction on par with calling an invasion and occupation a "war of liberation." However, despite a relentless propaganda campaign, *Jihad* does not mean "holy war." The word, deriving from the Arabic root *j-h-d*, means "to strive or struggle."[1] In Islamic tradition, there are five forms of *Jihad*, and indeed, one of them means to take up arms ... in *defense* of one's people and way of life. But the form that most resonates with me is *Jihad bil-qalam*: "to strive by means of the pen."

And what is it that one strives for in *Jihad bil-qalam*? ... The truth.

This book represents just that. It is a record of the struggle of many individuals in the mid-Michigan region who, through their writing, are seeking to illuminate the truth. In a world where the boardrooms of corporate-owned media are indistinguishable from the those of oil companies and weapons manufacturers (both of which are indistinguishable from the Cabinet of the current administration), this struggle is never easy. It requires the courage to put forth unpopular truths in the midst of popular lies. It requires the determination to ask the questions that we're warned shouldn't be asked. It requires the strength to be ridiculed, insulted, threatened, and shunned by those who are unable or unwilling to see through the rhetoric of fear and hate espoused by all those who profit by our acquiescence and silence.

The writings herein take many forms: poetry, letters, essays, speeches, fiction, teach-in lectures held at Saginaw Valley State University, and statements released by Tri-City Action for Peace (TCAP). They cover a range of topics from Iraq and Palestine to support for troops and responding to terror. But for all their variety, they have a common thread: a deep commitment to fostering a community, nation, and world of non-violence and justice; and the courage, determination, and strength to continue the struggle, to tirelessly strive for truth, for as long as necessary. Which is why that with the penning of these words, this book may be finished, but the greater work it represents is ongoing: Our struggle is a work in progress.

–MB
Saginaw, MI; 11/03

---

[1] Syracuse University College of Law Fact Sheet on Islam and Jihad.

Contents

Responding to the Response:

9/11 and the Peace Community

Cocoon

by Kathryn Emmenecker Muenzer

The most precious days of summer
often come after Labor Day
and that's how it was that morning
in New York City and Saginaw, MI.
Achingly blue sky usurped
by surreal imbedded airplane, a billow of smoke.
I spent the day in our basement,
because that's where our TV is.
All eyes riveted on the World Trade Center,
sterile towers of Mammon, its vertical lines
symbol of the American dollar.

No longer surreal puzzle – what did we do
to make someone that angry?
The fleeting realization that "Dubya"
would have his own war,
and it's going to be bigger than daddy's.

But it was not a day for politics, not a day for thinking.
Human tragedy demanded our hearts –
the nameless, the torched, the crushed, the jumpers,
rescue workers, police and firemen
climbing stairs to certain death.

Our country was in shock, first reaction
to disaster, crises. Some of us stayed focused
on a television set once banished to the basement,
others, wiser perhaps, turned off the TV,
realizing there was nothing anyone could do.

But our President appeared fully in control,
vengeance demanded, dissent unpatriotic,
Congress, perhaps still in their own shock,
voted money, relinquished power.
It was the patriotic thing to do.

A nation silenced, unquestioning,
ignorant of peace rallies, of anti-war protests
(ignored or blacked out by major TV networks).
Timid dissenters spun our own cocoon
of fear, frustration and anger – then crawled inside.

Fascism on Our Street Corners
by Marc Beaudin

For the past two evenings, a small group of people have stood on a corner near the Saginaw Court House displaying the worst possible reaction to the horrible tragedy of the 11th. These people wave flags and yell (sometimes with obscenities) at passing drivers to honk their horns. The banner they carry reads, "Americans, Let's Go to War. There are no innocent civilians anymore." Smaller signs urge us to "show them we mean it."

This eruption of hatred is worse than a policy of "an eye for an eye," since it seeks not merely the suffering of the guilty, but the suffering of all the people falling into these zealots' definition of "them." One banner-carrier defined "them" in part as "Libya, Iran, Iraq, and Afghanistan." It seems that being middle eastern and/or Islamic is a crime worthy of death in these people's minds.

This condemning as evil all the people born into nations, cultures, and religions shared by a handful of terrorists is exactly the mindset held by those very terrorists who must believe that all Americans are guilty by association of the crimes of the U.S. government. Indeed, by their blind hatred and lust for blood, the people waving their banners and flags on Court Street are aligning themselves with the very terrorists that they hate. Answering evil with evil only aids the growth of this horrible cancer.

Obviously, the criminals behind this atrocity must be found and brought to justice, but to allow one terrible act to merely inspire more of them is not only wrong, but a profound insult to the memory of those who have died. Does anyone really believe that they would want their deaths avenged by slaughtering more innocents?

What I witnessed this evening was not a show of patriotism, but fascism. I felt that I had gone back in time and was watching the birth of the Nazi party, and I sincerely hope that the majority of us will stand against violence and murder whether it comes from "them" or "us."

The High Road
by Monique Metcalf

I am very fortunate to be visiting this amazing country that is the United States of America. Before I left South Africa, where I live, I remember listening to Neil Diamond's song "Coming to America," and feeling the excitement bubbling through me. This is after all, the greatest nation on Earth.

I have visited several beautiful American cities, but Washington, DC certainly left the deepest impression on me. I am not American, but I could not stop myself from trembling–nor could I stop the tears as I walked through Arlington Cemetery, silently stood before the Vietnam Memorial, and contemplated the Korean War Memorial.

I urge President Bush to not make a decision that could lead to even one more white stone in Arlington Cemetery. Please do not let there be another opportunity for a war memorial. Please do not send even one more American son to be massacred in a war.

President Bush stands at a major crossroads right now, with an enormous amount of responsibility on his shoulders. The prayers of people around the world are with him, urging him to make the right decision. As the most powerful man on the planet, and with the money, technology and information available, the president has the power to change the course of history. He has the opportunity to recreate this world, put an end to the fighting, feed the hungry and save the planet.

I pray Bush will find the courage to take the road less traveled. I hope he will become a world leader whose name is mentioned with those of Mahatma Gandhi, Martin Luther King Jr. and Nelson Mandela: men who had the courage to change the world without violence. I pray that Bush will be surrounded by people who will encourage and support him in this difficult time.

I know that the American people, and indeed, all the people in the world, will support President Bush in taking the higher road that will lead to peace, harmony and good will in the world.

Shredding the Fragile Thread of Goodwill
by Leo R. Lynch

The citizens of ancient Rome coined a sardonic saying: *quod non fecerunt barbari fecerunt Barberini*. Freely translated that means: what the barbarians did not get around to destroying, the Barberini family did. This family was notorious for pillaging the art treasures of Rome and using them to enhance the beauty of Roman church buildings.

Today we can substitute "terrorists" for barbarians and the Bush administration for the Barberini. What the so-called terrorists didn't get round to destroying on September 11, 2001, the Bushies have done a good job of obliterating. One of the most precious things they have squandered is the opportunity, after 9/11, for our country to stand tall and demonstrate that we were capable of building on a reservoir of international sympathy and solidarity expressed by countries throughout the world. Instead, the president and his chief advisors, Vice-President Cheney and Donald Rumsfeld in particular, have been hell-bent on waging war–a war that seemingly has no more precise focus than the elimination of terrorists and the destruction of countries which harbor terrorists. In so doing they have managed to dissipate whatever feelings of empathy other countries, including Iran, showed the American people. Bush shredded that fragile thread of good will when he announced his ill-fated intention of going after terrorists in the so-called "axis of evil."

Bush's shameless pronouncements about preserving freedom in the world are belied by the brazen robbery of civil rights under the imperious Attorney General John Ashcroft, whose reckless and unchallenged dismantling of the Constitution and the Bill of Rights is obvious to anyone willing to take a look. Rumsfeld's effort to justify the unilateral decision of the Bush administration to invade Iraq has been duplicitous and misleading. How members of Congress cannot see through such sophomoric responses as Rumsfeld's to the charge of "where's the smoking gun?" is incredible. The question is a rhetorical way of asking where is the credible evidence for all the charges the administration is hurling at Hussein. The answer is that there is little hard evidence– merely speculation–proffered by the administration. This is just another version of the Bush administration's imperial admonition to the American people: trust us, don't badger us for facts.

The Bush response to the Iraqi acquiescence to weapons inspections makes it very clear that this administration doesn't want peace. It is bound and determined to take our country into war. Unfortunately, given a pusillanimous Congress and blatant support and cooperation of our media, it is more than likely that they will succeed.

The Unnamed Woman:
A Few Scattered Pieces
by Helen Raica-Klotz

Piece One: The Other
Do not be mistaken.
Just because my name is not recorded in your sacred texts
does not mean I was not real,
not flesh and blood.

I lived then, and I do now.
You have only a piece of my story, but I am so much more than these
pieces.

I am your grandmother,
    back curved over the kitchen sink, arms deep in the soapy water.
I am your daughter,
    sleeping underneath a faded quilt, face slack-jawed and warm.
I am your mother,
    hair spilled forward in her eyes, hands curved around a newborn
child.
I am your sister,
    lips parting ever so slightly, cheek turning toward a lover's caress.
I am your neighbor,
    kneeling in her garden, coaxing the chamomile to grow high and
yellow in the sun.

I live, not just on the page,
but in the shadows of all your lives,
waiting to step into the light and be seen, be heard, be recognized.

Piece Two: The Me
By losing my name
I become anyone – any one of you.
Do not be deceived
or keep me at arms distance.
You and I are separated only by the twist of fate's hand

       the subtle difference of time
       or gender
       or social class
Differences that are always razor thin,
that can turn on a dime.

But you know this.
I can see it in your eyes.
You too have had parts of you torn away,
pieces of your soul ripped asunder
irretrievable losses that cannot be whispered,
even in the dark.

The pain comes, it always does,
spoken aloud or hushed into silence.
We are a broken people, you and I.
Come, let us keen together.

Piece Three: The Us
So what is the story?

I was raped and beaten by men
who held a little power and a great deal of fear.

I lay on your doorstep every morning.
You find me when daylight comes.
My eyes are blackened, my robes are bloodstained and torn.

What do you say? How does the ending unfold?

Do you cut me into pieces -
send parts of me to the nations -
demand restitution -
rage at Evil and Your Enemies and other abstract nouns,
and try to cover up your own frailty of spirit and cruelty of heart?

Or do you simply lift me to your bosom,
press your fingers into my flesh to staunch my wounds,
rock me in your arms,
and weep softly for our losses,
which are always collective, never singular?

(Author's Note: This text is based on the beating, gang rape, and eventual murder of a female concubine described in Judges 19, a woman who is never named and seldom preached about. In this biblical story, a man spends the night in an unfamiliar village when a gang of men come to the door and demand the stranger to come out so that they "may have intercourse with him." The man, frightened, sends out his concubine instead, who is repeatedly beaten and raped throughout the night. In the morning, the master finds the woman lying on the doorstep, takes her home, and cuts her body into twelve pieces, sending her body parts to the twelve tribes of Israel, demanding restitution for the treatment of this concubine. In the ensuing war, over 900,000 men are killed.)

Calling for Sanity:

Seeking to Counter the Buildup to War

We Refuse to Be Intimidated
by Dr. Judith B. Kerman

There are more reasons to oppose the war the United States is pursuing in Iraq than I can take time to list, but I want to start by mentioning the one I consider the most important. By attacking a country which cannot be considered by any reasonable standard to have threatened us directly, the Bush administration will throw away international law. They will demonstrate that the US considers itself entitled to decide for the world what is good for the world. They will give aid and comfort to the enemies of our country, who can then point to our actions as proof of what they already thought–that the US is a bully, a rogue nation.

The US government has thrown away its moral legitimacy. In the Declaration of Independence, the founders of our democracy declared that a "decent respect for the opinions of others" required that they explain their decision to declare independence. It is clear that the Bush administration has a level of contempt for the respect of other nations, even our long-standing and stalwart allies, unprecedented in US history. What is more, this contempt has been expressed in language worthy of the elementary school playground, as much as saying "if you don't agree with whatever I say, I'll knock your crayons on the floor." I don't want to understate the probable impact of American violence on Iraqi civilians, but I'd like to focus on the underlying issues, especially the domestic US political context in which this proposed war is developing.

We are in great danger as a democracy, and it's essential that we be clear about the stakes. Right after September 11, President Bush declared to the world that the terrorists hate the US because they hate our freedoms. Yet the Bush administration has been working energetically since that time to take those freedoms away. They are using both intimidation and legal strategies that damage basic Constitutional rights: the right to a speedy trial, the right to legal counsel, the right to confront your accuser and even to know what you are accused of. The administration claims it can take those rights away anytime it decides someone is an enemy combatant, a "terrorist," even when that person is a US citizen. Already there is talk of this label being applied to gang members in inner cities, adding the threat of total deprivation of civil rights to the problems of racism, economic disinvestments, hopelessness and poverty in our cities. Under the proposed legal regime, a "terrorist" would have little more legal protection than slaves did before the Civil

War. As free men and women, we must speak out against these abuses, and the mindset that proposes them. Speaking out is frightening, but we must refuse to be intimidated.

Freedom of speech means whether or not the government likes what we say. Freedom of assembly and the press means whether or not the government likes what we say. Upholding those rights is the very nature of freedom. We must refuse to be intimidated.

Ever since September 11, the Bush administration has been trying frantically to find someone to punish. The US attacked Afghanistan. Has it made us safer? Has anyone figured out where Osama Bin Laden is? Is Afghanistan now a stable country that does not breed or shelter terrorists? Is there serious journalism coming out of Afghanistan to tell us? Where are the headlines? Suddenly it's Iraq. Next, maybe North Korea. Or Iran. Our government, although we did not elect its leaders, is claiming the right to impose its ideas of democracy wherever it chooses. A major effort is being made to distract us. And people who object to the administration's adventures are accused of being unpatriotic. Expressing dissent is not unpatriotic, it is the essence of patriotism. We refuse to be intimidated.

President Bush, Vice-President Cheney, Attorney General Ashcroft, Secretary of Defense Rumsfeld and their cronies want to keep the attention of the American people distracted from the real issues. The real issues all over the world are peace, freedom, social justice, reversing the damage we are doing to the planet. If freedom means anything, it means the freedom of people to choose the government and the social system that will serve them best. Let me hear you say it with me: We refuse to be intimidated.

The multinational corporations that put George Bush and his friends into power are riddled with mismanagement, corruption and criminal behavior. The US refuses to cooperate in international efforts to stop environmental damage. The administration wants to lower taxes on the rich and the corporations even further. Meanwhile the Bush administration panders to corporate greed and tries to roll back 50 years of painful progress toward social justice. And they call that freedom. We know better. Please say it with me: we refuse to be intimidated.

A war against a bogeyman is always a great way to distract people. Saddam Hussein is a bloodthirsty tyrant–no doubt about it. But the US government has protected or installed many bloodthirsty tyrants over many years, all over the world. In fact, the US was partly responsible for Hussein's being in power. Now George W. Bush needs an enemy that he knows he can find and defeat. Saddam Hussein is an easy target. He's also left-over business from George Bush the First. A cheap victory, except for the Iraqi civilians who have been suffering for years. And when we raise doubts about the wisdom of this adventure we are accused of being unpatriotic. Let me hear it: We refuse to be intimidated.

Passover is coming soon. Then Jews all over the world will celebrate the Exodus from Egypt, the emergence from slavery into freedom. That story has inspired people all over the world with a vision of freedom. But freedom cannot be won by bombing Iraq. It cannot be won by manipulating the governments of other nations. It cannot be won by refusing to negotiate or increasing the misery of civilians. It cannot be won by unilateral military action against the advice of America's allies. As the Prophet wrote: Not by might, not by power, but by my Spirit, says the Lord of Hosts. Let me hear it: We refuse to be intimidated.

People all over the world are protesting against this war. They do not hate the United States. They resist the Bush Doctrine, the idea that the US government is free to impose its will by force anywhere and anytime. That may be what George Bush means by freedom, but it's not what we mean by it. Let's all shout it together: We refuse to be intimidated.

[This speech was originally presented as part of a TCAP rally at Bourchard Park in Saginaw. Later versions were given at both Teach-ins held at Saginaw Valley State University. –Editor]

Use Diplomacy to Seek Peace

by Georgeen d'Haillecourt, C. Peter Dougherty, and Joan McCoy

Since the beginning of the Gulf War, the Iraqi citizens have suffered at US hands. Even since the last bomb was dropped in Iraq, the violence has continued with the sanctions being used as weapons of economic mass destruction, victimizing innocent civilians.

Just as things were beginning to look better, here we go again. To quote Um Marwan of Baghdad, as reported in *USA Today*, "Clinton's missiles are hitting every Iraqi in the heart and we the ordinary people are the victims. I hate him, hate him, hate him. Why is he taking our food away?"

As US citizens, we also ask "Why?"–giving rise to our questions:

Did Saddam Hussein violate the sanctions? Did the US intervene in a civil war? Why are the allies split over this action? Why now? Is this a political move? Is the US testing the "new and improved" cruise missile? Is the United States going to spill more blood for oil?

While the sanctions are immoral, the present attack by the United States is obscene. Neither do we condone the violence of Saddam Hussein. As people of peace, we continue to condemn violence on all sides in this conflict and call for resolution through nonviolent diplomacy.

[*This letter was written in 1996 and refers to the first Gulf War and the sanctions and bombings that continued throughout the Clinton years. Although it predates most of the material of this collection, it serves as a reminder of just how long the Iraqi people have been suffering at the hands of the US.* –Editor]

Regime Change Vital
by Marc Beaudin

Liberty, democracy, and justice are being threatened, indeed attacked, by a man representing powerful forces of greed and repression. It is the duty of every freedom-loving person to work to stop this man and his agenda.

He not only possesses weapons of mass destruction, including chemical, biological, and nuclear, but has openly stated a willingness to use them; claiming a right to use "any means available" to kill his enemies.

He has invaded other nations, killing thousands of civilians, and leaving millions more to suffer in starvation, homelessness, and the hazards of environmental destruction.

He has imprisoned hundreds of his own people without due process or disclosure.

He has closed off his country from the community of nations by insulting and ignoring the policies of the United Nations; refusing to support world treaties ranging from child labor laws to environmental protections; and attempting to force other nations, against their own laws and the will of their people, to accept his nation's trade rules.

This man again and again has shown himself to be an enemy of peace, a ruthless leader of a rogue state, and a greed-driven egomaniac. Worst of all is the fact that he was not even elected by the people of his nation: he was appointed by a handful of conservative members of his elite class.

The time for decisive action is now. A regime change in the United States is vital: Oust Bush before it's too late.

The US Once Helped Arm Iraq, but Today Demands Disarmament-Why?
by Christine Genualdi

According to senior military officers, the Reagan administration "provided Iraq with critical battle planning assistance at a time when American intelligence agencies knew that Iraqi commanders would employ chemical weapons in waging the decisive battles of the Iran-Iraq war."[1] Wait! Why would the US help Iraq use chemical weapons? Well, in the decade before the Gulf War, the US sold chemical weapons to Iraq and taught Iraq how to use them as part of the secretly US-supported Iraqi war against Iran. A *New York Times* article states that in the 1980's the US provided Iraq "with satellite intelligence so that Iraq could use chemical weapons against Iranian soldiers" and that the US "shipped seven strains of anthrax to Iraq between 1978 and 1988."[2]

Why is there practically no mention today how the US armed Saddam? The Bush administration recently said that the US needs to invade Iraq and gain full control over the state so the US can "carry out their principle mission: finding and destroying weapons of mass destruction."[3] Bush tells the nation that Iraq "stands alone as a threat, armed with weapons of mass destruction controlled by a murderous tyrant."[4] He instills fear in Americans that Saddam has all these weapons and is capable of mass killings. But he fails to mention how the US sold these same weapons to Saddam and helped him integrate them into Iraqi battle plans. And he also fails to mention how US corporations and stockholders profited from these sales. So in the 1980s, the US profited by creating the "murderous tyrant" who now is considered a threat to the US. Why doesn't the US take any of this blame? Why does Iraq have to take all the blame while US corporations get rich? It's no

---

[1]Tyler, Patrick E. "Officers Say US Aided Iraq in War Despite Use of Gas." *The New York Times*, August 18, 2002.

[2]Kristof, Nicolas D. "Revolving-Door Monsters." *The New York Times*, October 11, 2002.

[3]Sanger, David E. and Eric Schmitt. "US Has a Plan to Occupy Iraq, Officials Report." *The New York Times*, October 11, 2002, pp A1, A14.

[4]Hulse, Carl and Alison Mitchell. "CIA Says Attack May Ignite Terror." *The New York Times*, October 9, 2002, pp A1, A12.

shock that Iraq has all these weapons: as House Representative Slaughter says, "Sure [Hussein] has biological weapons, we gave them to him."[1]

So the president says we need to invade Iraq in order to destroy the very same weapons that the US once gave Iraq and helped Iraq to use. This doesn't make too much sense; what is the real reason? First we must understand what Bush wants to do under this guise. An article in the *New York Times* describes the tentative plan for Iraq: the US wants to "install an American-led military government in Iraq if the United States topples Saddam Hussein."[2] So the US plans to violate Iraq's sovereignty and overthrow the present government. But what gives the US the right to do this? Supposedly the claim that Iraq is a possible threat to the US, but even the CIA thinks the probability of Iraqi threat is low and feels that if Mr. Hussein feels a US attack imminent, "he probably would become much less constrained in adopting terrorist actions."[3] Wait a minute, isn't the US supposed to be fighting a war against terrorism, trying to decrease threats of terrorist attacks? This still doesn't make sense. But then why does Bush feel that using force on Iraq will help to "build a future of security and peace for ourselves and for the world?"[4]

Perhaps he is trying to instill fear in the American people so they will support his unjustified war on Iraq. It is no coincidence that on September 12, 2002, Bush visited the UN to tell them they should "stand up to Saddam Hussein, demand inspections for the weapons of mass destruction and remove or destroy them."[5] Of all days, why did he pick the day after 9/11, a time of national mourning and thus patriotism? Perhaps he remembers this time last year when his popularity grew overnight as the American people were stricken with fear and grief and many felt a renewed sense of patriotism, and thus support of their country, government, and president. Most were in high support of the once controversial president and his ironic war on terrorism. So if Bush wanted to start another war, again, now would be a good time. All he

---

[1] Hulse.

[2] Sanger.

[3] Hulse.

[4] Loven, Jennifer. Associated Press, September 29, 2002.

[5] Senators Daschle, Durbin, Gramm, and Warner. "Excerpts from the Senate Debate on Authorizing Use of Force in Iraq." *The New York Times*, October 11, 2002, p A14.

needs to do is to instill fear in the American people and connect this war to the war on terrorism so they will support him. And in my opinion, that's exactly what the Bush administration and supporting corporations are doing, and this is evident in the media.

The media are controlled by a small number of huge and wealthy corporations so often the information we receive has somewhat of a corporate bias. Corporations often donate large sums of money to political campaigns and thus have an influence on government policy. So corporations and government policy go hand-in-hand, and if they will benefit from war on Iraq, they will probably try to gain support of the public through the media.

I have seen the newspapers try to make a connection between war on Iraq and the war on terrorism, because if the people who support the war on terrorism see a connection, they will be likely to support a war on Iraq. In one article, Bush mentions that "each passing day could be the one in which the Iraqi regime gives anthrax or VX nerve gas or someday a nuclear weapon to a terrorist group"[1] But this is such an empty statement, with no backing of evidence or research; more so, it's political propaganda. Any country could be giving weapons to terrorist groups, and this statement is just a guess of the future, the only evidence being that Iraq has biological weapons. Well, so do many other states. So Bush and the media are trying to make this connection between Iraq and terrorism, but why go through all the trouble just to gain public support? What do the Bush administration and US corporations have to gain by invading Iraq?

I think the answer to that question is oil. *The Saginaw News* mentioned that "if the Bush administration makes good on threats to overthrow Iraqi leader Saddam Hussein, one consequence could be a return of cheap Iraqi oil to the market."[2] Finally the real connection between invasion of Iraq and oil is made. Think for a moment, why did the US choose Iraq? I'm sure many other countries have weapons of mass destruction, potentially dangerous leaders, and a possibility that such weapons would fall in the hands of terrorist groups. The reason is because Iraq has oil, lots of it, at least 112 billion barrels in reserve, and "there's not an oil company out there that wouldn't be interested in

---

[1]Loven.

[2]Helicke, James C. "Oil Pipeline Could Change Mideast Links." *The Saginaw News*, October 12, 2002, p A8.

24

Iraq."[1] This oil is currently unavailable to US corporations because of UN sanctions.

So after the US invades Iraq, the White House plans to "put an American officer in charge of Iraq for a year or more while the United States and its allies searched for weapons and maintained Iraq's oil fields."[2] Wait, what do chemical weapons have to do with oil fields? Is the US afraid Mr. Hussein is going to poison Americans with oil? I don't think so. The article mentions that because the US will be waging war in Iraq, eventually Iraq will have to undergo "stabilization and reconstruction" and will be in need of funds to do so, so the US will implement an "oil for food program." Wow, there's a bright idea, if we want oil, we can destroy a country so then they must sell their oil to us in order to have food to survive. Ingenious! But why do we want this oil so bad that we're willing to risk our soldiers' lives and kill Iraqi soldiers and civilians, bringing destruction to their nation?

One reason is there is a lot of money to be made with this oil, for oil companies and their stockholders, and other businesses that profit from cheap Iraqi oil. Also, the top government officials will profit from Iraq's oil. "Bush and Vice President Cheney have worked in the oil business and have long-standing ties to the industry."[3] Cheney used to be chief executive of Halliburton from 1995-2000, until he became vice president. So the big guys on top who are trying to convince the public to invade Iraq will personally gain while US soldiers and Iraqi soldiers and citizens lose their lives. Does this seem fair and reasonable to you?

---

[1] Morgan, Dan and David Ottaway,. "In Iraq War Scenario, Oil is Key Issue." WashingtonPost.com.

[2] Sanger.

[3] Morgan.

Justice, Mercy, and Humility
by Morgan Guyton

The Hebrew prophet Micah has advice for Americans concerned about our global image as a bully. Predicting God's destruction of Israel because of a corrupt government and religious establishment, Micah said it could be averted through atonement and repentance. "Will the Lord be pleased with thousands of rams, with ten thousand rivers of oil?" he asks a people who thought they could buy forgiveness. No Micah answers, "Act justly, love mercy, and walk humbly with your God" (Micah 6: 7-8).

Justice, mercy, and humility should be the three cornerstones of our country's foreign policy, instead of buying friendships and cutting short-term deals according to economic interests. Saddam Hussein was the third largest recipient of US military aid in 1984 when we arm-wrestled the Soviet Union for his friendship. Since our past foreign relations have had ulterior economic motives, we will need to show humility before we earn the global trust to pursue justice and mercy. Our president would do well to read the book of Micah.

Dawn, Dec. 15, 2002
by Patricia McNair

Seven forty-five, black branches appear
against a night-blue sky.
I am reading poetry by Naomi Shihab Nye.
She writes of war in Palestine,
an Iraqi woman feeding her ducks
in America, saddened by war
between her two countries.

As dawn slowly reveals my yard,
the neighbor's swing set, the bird bath,
I read more poems. This writer
is half American, half Middle Eastern.
There is never despair in her words
only truth of how women feel
when food is scarce, bombs shock,
no one has parties any more.

The sky becomes a pale blue,
winter grass shows dull green,
the clock ticks. It's Sunday morning.
These poems were published in 1998.
How many days have dawned since then?
How many women still suffer in the Middle East?
Moment by moment the light changes ...

Response to the State of the Union (2002)
by Tri-City Action for Peace

President Bush's address gave no new evidence supporting his case for a war against Iraq. All assertions he made regarding Iraq's obstruction of weapons inspections, support for the al-Qaeda international terrorist network, and pursuit of weapons of mass destruction have been made in the past and debunked by international authorities. If Bush did have new evidence, he should have presented it to the American people and the world in his public address rather than claim that Colin Powell would reveal all at a future meeting of United Nations officials.

President Bush cast the conflict between the US and Iraq as a "contest of will, perseverance, and power." We believe this is the wrong attitude to have when facing a difficult decision that will result in the loss of millions of innocent lives. It is not willpower but honesty and humility that should be the cornerstones of one's attitude toward war. The value of American lives is not greater than that of Iraqi lives. It is unacceptable to risk their innocent deaths to prevent the remote possibility of American lives being lost. Furthermore, a war against Iraq will increase the likelihood of terrorist retaliation.

We are not swayed by the politics of fear in this State of the Union address. President Bush made reference to an "ideology of power and domination" that has "appeared again" in our world. Like most of the phrases he used to describe Saddam Hussein, we believe this categorizes the attitude of *our* president. Bush arrogantly described America as being "God's gift to humanity." Like the original doctrine of manifest destiny, this statement fails to justify America's pursuit of world dominance.

When describing the extra-judicial killing of terrorists, Bush said that they had learned "the meaning of American justice." That may be "American justice" to him but we believe that true justice seeks not to destroy but rather to reconcile humanity. We strongly support the pursuit of global justice, which we take to mean the reordering of power relationships and resources to enable human rights and dignity for all people on this planet. Only this kind of justice will dismantle the power of international terrorism and enable the true reconciliation of humanity and true global peace.

Insane Path

by Leo R. Lynch

This is in regard to two headlines that appeared January 17 in a Michigan daily newspaper. The first headline read: "War talk gets state's pacifists moving." The word pacifist simply means one who is opposed to war. However, it generally carries a lot of negative freight, with huge implications of cowardice and lack of patriotism. As a word for people like me who are opposed to President George W. Bush's efforts to carry us into war with Iraq, it is woefully inadequate.

Let me make the connection with the other headline: "A man of his word: Poet Sekou Sundiata inspires young writers to find their voices." The article describes the efforts of a black poet to help young black students find their voices through poetry.

Sound a bit far-fetched? Not really. The root from which the word poetry is derived means "to make something that springs from vision, imagination and creativity." Sundiata makes positive assumptions about his young charges: He assumes they are capable of becoming poets–people of vision, imagination and creativity.

Pacifists are, at heart, poets. They believe that there are healthier alternatives to bombing other nations and killing thousands of innocent women and children. Pacifists believe, as do poets, that miracles can be worked with vision, imagination and creativity.

During the past few months, these qualities have been woefully and shamefully lacking in this administration's approach to Saddam Hussein and the Iraqi people. This administration has for months displayed a shameful and pitiful lack of talent for diplomacy and statesmanship. They have demonstrated little interest in exercising vision, imagination and creativity. Little wonder. When you have the biggest weapons of mass destruction in your arsenal while declaring others you deem as evil should not have them, you are convinced you can have your way no matter what world opinion says.

There are no pacifists in this administration. Neither are there any poets. To be a poet demands honesty and integrity, qualities this administration holds in low regard. A few months ago we heard President Bush claim that a study by the International Atomic Energy Agency showed that Iraq could produce a nuclear capability within six months. Guess what? The agency never issued such a report. And this is the man who wants us to march blindly into war with Iraq?

Our lives must bespeak who we are. Our lives must bespeak what we believe in. We must continue to dream a better world. We must lay claim to being poets as well as pacifists.

That is the only hope for a country and a world that appear headed down the insane path of war and destruction.

US Risks Best, Brightest
by Dr. Margot Haynes

It is with heavy heart that I write. With the disintegration of the space shuttle Columbia, we have lost seven of the best human beings produced by our world civilization. We mourn together as one world.

Yet the United States continues to send thousands upon thousands of our best American young people to the Middle East. They are ordered to prepare to engage in an unprovoked attack on a sovereign nation. Call it "preemptive strike" or "defensive offense," it still does not qualify as morally defensible under the guidelines of "just war." American religious leaders have bravely spoken out against this unjust war. It horrifies me to see my country's leaders place so many exemplary young people unnecessarily–and immorally–in harm's way.

But we are not only setting our soldiers up, so close to the center of strife and extremism, as sitting ducks for any terrorist's biological or chemical attack. We are also teaching others around the globe that we are a bullying nation ready to use our outsized power to enforce our will, regardless of the view of other nations.

How are we to win respect from those abroad: young people pulled by the temptations of extremism in their own land, patriotic toward their own countries, fearful of the US arsenal of weapons of mass destruction (greater atomic power than any other nation on Earth, which of late our leaders have threatened to use "preemptively")?

Our country can win this war only by keeping the respect it has held around the world, by extending that respect more deeply in the lands of the extremists. Christopher Bassford, professor of strategy at our National War College in Washington, DC, shocked me by saying that if the Cold War was equivalent to "World War III," then what we are planning now is "World War IV." He does not seem to think our approach makes sense: "Genuine victory ... will be won in the markets of Afghanistan, the streets of Palestine, private homes in Iraq, and the churches and mosques of America itself" (*The Saginaw News*, 22 Jan. 2003).

Bassford criticizes our leaders' call to a War on Terrorism. "Wars are fought over political disagreement, not against a technique of applying violence. Declaring a 'war on terrorism' is like declaring 'war on carrier aviation' after December 7, 1941." Bassford calls this conflict "an ideological struggle for the soul of the human race, one we very well could lose."

I believe we can win it by acting with justice and morality. We must build respect around the world for our wisdom, for our restraint and for the patience needed to work slowly toward negotiated solutions. Bullying threats require us to place our patriotic and well-trained young people in the face of the gravest danger.

This approach is likely to lead to their deaths and martyrdom; further national mourning without building a safer world.

Letter to George W. Bush
by William P. Stone

Dear President Bush:

I am writing to let you know that I am not in support of war with Iraq. I cannot sit and idly watch without comment.

I am a Christian. I believe in Jesus as the Christ. And, for most of my adult life, I have been a Republican. I am a Quality Engineer, certified by the American Society for Quality. As a quality professional, I have been taught to define problems completely, immediately contain the problem, understand the root cause(s) and to address the root cause(s) with corrective action(s).

The idea of war, especially with Iraq, goes against my belief in God and his commands, my professional teachings and practices, and, ultimately, erodes my support of the Republican Party.

As I started to think of what this war might mean, and how, as a quality professional, I would address it, I started thinking of what is a justifiable situation for war.

Justification might be an outgrowth of some actions so heinous, so vile, and so against all human values, that the only possibility to change the behavior is war. Maybe, just maybe, that is just. The removal of Hitler from Europe in World War II is, in those terms, justified.

But, have the acts of Iraq been acts justifying war?

The attack of September 11th was not done by Iraq. It wasn't even conducted by a country but rather by a fanatical group.

The beginning of the current specter wasn't the horrific events of September 11th. It wasn't the Gulf War. It wasn't sanctions. It is, in fact, not simply one activity or event. Rather, it is the totality of all these events and more, that has instilled hate, ignorance and distrust.

To eliminate the source of a problem, an understanding of the problem and its root cause is necessary. Therefore, from a quality perspective, let's look at the problem, as it faces us today.

First, the attacks of September 11th, though horrible and unconscionable, weren't acts of war. They were the acts of people who hate. They were acts of people who don't know the targeted people. They were acts of people who do not trust the motives of those targeted.

Early in the attacks' aftermath, reports in the United States media opined that the goal was the collapse of the American economy. The lack of understanding was never clearer. Causing a building to collapse, killing innocent people, won't bring about real change in economies. If we look at our response to September 11th, what would make us believe that the same type of acts, bombings and all other war atrocities, will bring about a change of heart in those who don't understand us?

The hatred that drove the attacks of September 11th is clear. The lack of understanding is certainly clear. But what of the credibility of the United States? How are we viewed elsewhere?

If we hadn't tried to push our weight around in Vietnam, or Panama, or Grenada ... and on and on from there, people, worldwide, would have a different view of the United States. If we hadn't propped up dictators or military regimes, to further our agendas, if we had truly followed up our words with actions, then the people of the world, outside of the United States, would view us differently.

So I define the problem description for September 11th more like this, "The attacks of September 11th were the malicious actions of people driven by hate, ignorance and distrust."

Joseph C. Wilson, chief of mission at the United States Embassy in Baghdad from 1988 to 1991 and acting ambassador during Operation Desert Shield, believes the goals of the United States are unclear. Is the goal liberation of Iraq's people, another step in the "war" on terrorism, or disarming Iraq? No matter what or how eloquent the statement of Secretary of State Colin Powell, the case for war isn't clear.

Liberation of People

Why only Iraq? Is the United States going to begin a campaign to go around the world making changes as it sees fit without the support of the United Nations?

War on Terrorism

Again, Joseph C. Wilson argues that any "assertion that Saddam might share weapons of mass destruction with a terrorist group, however, is counterintuitive to everything I and others know about him." Mr. Wilson believes that Saddam can only lose through direct involvement with the terrorists.

Disarming Iraq

Saddam, according to Mr. Wilson, believes that the United States is intent, not only on disarming Saddam and Iraq, but also killing Saddam.

None of these, liberation, terrorism or disarming, successfully addresses hatred, ignorance or distrust. Liberation is the responsibility of the Iraqi people. Terrorism is only reinforced through war. The Israel/Palestine example provides a convincing argument against war.

Disarming can be accomplished without war and with the backing of the United Nations. There isn't an indication that Saddam will easily comply, nor is there an indication that a strong show of force isn't needed. However, war isn't the only solution.

Looking again at what solves a problem, and accepting that war isn't the answer for eliminating hatred, ignorance or distrust, what of the root causes for hatred, ignorance and distrust?

To address hatred, if we are the Christian country of which we speak, we would show love rather than hate. War doesn't show love. War doesn't determine who is right; it determines who loses. Some lose less, but no one wins.

To address ignorance do you act as you always have? Do you work to build bridges or work to tear them down?

Can trust be built using negative words? By sponsoring hatred? By killing? Or bombing?

What do we do to address the problem? What is the root cause of this hate? Of this ignorance? Of this distrust?

War kills people. The innocent and the intended get the same deliberate dispatch. This killing will not reduce hatred. Therefore, we must find another alternative to eliminate hatred. One alternative is dialogue: open and honest dialogue.

By failing to work with our allies, friends and neighbors, we undermine a sacred trust we have. The United States is a citizen of this world. It is not the only country. It does not hold all the answers or solutions. And, the United States dares not undermine and effectively abolish the cohesive world body, the United Nations.

The use of prayers to the one true God (the same God worshiped by Jew, Muslim and Christian alike) that the United States be successful in war suggests that we are not being Christian. Mark Twain, writing of a war prayer, explained that anytime we ask God to make our side successful, we were also asking that the other side be unsuccessful. How can the same God who sent His Son to establish a new covenant based on love, give us His blessings to kill other people who worship and believe in Him? It just doesn't make sense.

Please find ways to make peace. Let us work, within God's world, with God's people for God's work. Let us not use the name of God for our vain purpose but lift ourselves up to do his work.

Sincerely,

William P. Stone

The True Terror
by Jason Graham

Another day has passed. Another act in the attempt to end terrorism has been tried and failed. The hatred of a vague enemy is shifted from border to border, from nationality to religion, from religion to idealism, and from oppressor to oppressed. Constantly our nation is drawn, by both fear and hatred, into engaging in this battle, feeling the rush of aggression–but never succeeding, never vanquishing this enemy of terror.

This is because the true terror is right here–not in front of the barrel but behind the trigger.

The terrifying enemy is only a reflection and you can't capture or vanquish a reflection. You can only run into its terrifying aggression over and over until you destroy both the self and the reflection, or change the acts of aggression from within.

The US demands that nations such as Iraq, Iran and North Korea are threats because of their development (or potential future development) of weapons of mass destruction, while our military leaders discuss the use of nuclear weapons, cruise missiles and a pre-emptive attack against the population of Iraq. We have more weapons, an infinitely greater amount of tax dollars going to the development of new weapons, and a more devastating history of using weapons of mass destruction than any country of the "axis of evil" could hope for.

We denounce countries for supporting or aiding terrorism. Yet we supported both Saddam and bin Laden during their most horrifying atrocities, only to stop when the weapons and finances we provided were turned against us or the interests of US corporations. We have financed or carried out acts of terrorism in East Timor, Guatemala, Nicaragua, Cuba, Palestine and Columbia that far outcry anything that our leaders demand that they are fighting against.

We condemn other countries as being "rogue" or unaccountable to the United Nations or the International Court of Justice (ICJ), while our government is stating that it will attack Iraq without their support or blessings. The US is also the only country to be condemned by the ICJ for acts of state terrorism–a condemnation we vetoed.

We are accusing other countries of lacking democracy while Bush just stated that he would still wage this war even with zero approval from the people of this country.

Which country has weapons of mass destruction? Which country is threatening violence, aggression, and warfare? Which country, time

35

after time, supported, contributed to, or created mass violence or acts of genocide?

Only by not acknowledging our reflection does our adversary take shape.

Only by being blind to ourselves does history fail to light the path to freedom and peace.

This is not a war on terror. It is a war *of* terror. Recognize it as such.

Powell Theatrics
by William A. Thibodeau

It was to be expected that *The Saginaw News* would promulgate
the Bush administration's propaganda and fear mongering following
Colin Powell's theatrics on the Iraq situation at the UN Security Council
("How many last chances?" Feb. 7, editorial).

But trying to discredit those who oppose the US war on Iraq by
saying, "... Nothing short of a photograph of Saddam straddling a
nuclear bomb ... would persuade some people," only suggests that *The
News'* motives in taking this position may be suspect.

All that is needed to persuade most anti-war folks that war is the
only way to deal with the monster Saddam are facts. These facts, not
myths, must prove that Iraq is an imminent, immediate threat to the
security of the United States.

In the eyes of those who have carefully studied and researched
the recent history of Iraq-US relations, the once respected Gen. Powell
has been reduced to a mythmaker. Accusations that the photos he
displayed revealed an Iraqi missile site and trucks carting away barrels
of chemical weapons before the inspectors arrived, were dismissed by
UN Chief Inspector Hans Blix and by journalists who visited these
locations to investigate.

The "missile site" had been monitored for months by the
inspection team and evidence of anything nuclear was nonexistent. As
for the trucks, none have been found in any of the more than 300
investigations.

The mythological Iraqi/al-Qaeda connection is another favorite
Bush administration accusation. The Central Intelligence Agency, as
recently as early February, has admitted that there is not one shred of
evidence to support this fantasy. Some al-Qaeda are known to be in
Northern Iraq fighting with the Kurdish rebels, but there is no contact
between the Iraqi government and that area because of the US-British
no-fly zone bombing.

Most people, including those opposed to war as the answer to
the Iraqi problem, accept the fact that Saddam Hussein is guilty of
numerous human rights violations and should be brought to account for
them.

For *The News* to repeat the standard accusation that the Iraqi
leader "gassed his own people" as though it were an act of genocide,
seems irresponsible and defies the facts. A CIA senior political analyst
during the Iran-Iraq war who was in charge of examining the evidence of

chemical weapons killing thousands of people in the Northern Iraqi town of Halabja, which had been captured by the Iranians at the end of that eight-year war, said the evidence proves that these tragic and morally repugnant bombings were acts of war. Iraq used chemical weapons to kill Iranians who had seized Halabja. The citizens of that town were not Iraq's main target.

The Bush administration has demonstrated that it is willing to resort to demagoguery to justify its war on the people of Iraq. *The Saginaw News* should have more respect for the intelligence and integrity of its readers.

Who Has Defended Our Freedom?

by Morgan Guyton

People often tell peace activists that we "attack" the military that "defends our freedom." We are called hypocrites for criticizing the institution which supposedly "won us" our right to criticize.

But who has our military defended us from in the years since Nazi Germany? Was it the Vietnamese who wanted freedom from French rule and puppet dictators? Was it the Nicaraguans who overthrew that ruthless tyrant Somoza who had given our government all the natural resources it wanted while bombing his own people? Bush has invested millions of advertising dollars to make you think our freedom is threatened by an Iraqi military decimated in the Gulf War and, through the sanctions ruthlessly imposed, prevented from rebuilding since then.

No conventional military invasion of the continental United States has occurred since 1814. That is why US civilians have no idea what devastation war does to a civilian population and why the claim that the military "defends our freedom" is so ludicrous.

Our freedoms have come through struggle since powerful white men have disrespected our Constitution throughout history. It was 1920 before women could vote thanks to freedom fighter Susan B. Anthony and others. It was 1956 before blacks could sit wherever they wanted on Alabama buses thanks to Rosa Parks and others. Your eight-hour workday came through the blood of union activists. Do not insult these heroes who worked hard for our freedom by crediting the military for their victories.

Request for a City Council Anti-War Resolution

by Tri-City Action for Peace

By way of this letter, members of the Saginaw community in favor of a peaceful resolution to the conflict with Iraq wish to invite you and the City Council to consider a resolution expressing your support for peaceful diplomacy. Ninety-three city councils across the country have already made this move, including Ann Arbor, Detroit, Ferndale, Traverse City, and Kalamazoo in Michigan.

Cities like ours need the federal government to spend its money on education, health care, and social services rather than military adventurism. Our economy is in a state of crisis and laid-off workers in Saginaw are struggling to feed their families due to the stinginess of the federal government's unemployment benefits. I have a good friend who is being denied Medicaid when it is the only way she can get treatment she must have before she will be able to work again. How can our government be so stingy and wasteful simultaneously?

A war against Iraq will have serious repercussions for our country's relationship with the rest of the world, where there is vociferous opposition to our war plans. If enough cities speak out for peace, perhaps Bush will honor the United Nations process which has thus far done an excellent job of slowly but surely disarming Saddam Hussein of any weapons of mass destruction and preventing him from using them on anyone.

Please read over this draft resolution and let us know if you have any suggested changes. We have carefully written it to be a principled statement that avoids unnecessary controversy. We are hoping the Council can consider this at its Monday meeting, which many people from Saginaw in favor of peace will be attending.

Thanks for your time.

[*On March 10, 2003, the Saginaw City Council, in a 6 to 1 vote, approved a resolution calling on President Bush and Congress to work with the United Nations and avoid a pre-emptive war against Iraq. The following two statements were among the many presented before the council before the vote was taken. –Editor*]

Address to Saginaw City Council
by Joe Locke

What is it that we wish to gain from a war against Iraq? If it's world peace, then we are definitely looking in the wrong direction. Look what happened to Iraq 12 years ago; people, especially women and children, are still suffering to this very day as result of the bombings and the sanctions placed upon them. Iraq can't handle another war. How can we support a war that will cause many more civilian deaths?

With the sanctions imposed on Iraq, even basic necessities such as medicine can't be brought into the country; water and sewage can't be treated because pipes and chemicals can't be brought in either; so many things we take for granted are unavailable for them. The US military, with its "Shock and Awe" plan will, within the first 48 hours of war, release 3,000 bombs and missiles all over the city of Baghdad. One Pentagon official said, "There won't be a safe place in Baghdad."

With millions around the world protesting and speaking out against this pre-emptive war, it is obvious the people do not want to see this war against Iraq come to be. Declaring such a pre-emptive war is going to turn countries against us, even our allies. The horrific images of innocent Iraqis being killed will not be seen on our television screens, but in the Middle East everyone will see them on al Jazeera. This will not help the image that Middle Easterners' have of the United States. They are already upset by Ariel Sharon and Israel's attacks on the Palestinians and the embargo imposed upon Iraq, which the United States so heavily insisted the UN put into effect.

If we are worrying about Saddam Hussein using biological or chemical weapons, then we must realize a brutal military bombardment on Iraq will only give him the reason to use them. Back in 1991, Saddam had the biological and chemical weapons to do great damage to United States, but he did not use them because he knew that he would be annihilated. He still knows that such a move would be suicide, and he isn't about to risk his power to do such a move. The only way he would use any sort of biological or chemical weaponry he might have is if we push him into a corner where he feels he has no other choice but to release them.

According to Colin Powell, Osama bin Laden and Saddam Hussein are supposedly linked together and Saddam might use that link to pass off any biological or chemical weaponry he might have. With a recent video of bin Laden speaking of his crusade, he called Saddam an "infidel" repeatedly, a term that he uses so frequently when speaking of the United States. In 1990, bin Laden actually offered to raise an army for Saudi Arabia to remove Iraq from Kuwait. The two were mortal enemies back then and still are to this very day.

We must keep in mind all who will die as result of this pending war on Iraq. How can we expect to bring forth peace when we are totally annihilating a city of 5 million people? In the end, it'll be the civilians, not Saddam Hussein, who'll suffer greatly by the attacks, even more greatly than they already do. I do not see how anyone can consciously support what appears to be an Iraqi genocide. All the war with Iraq will do is cause great suffering and breed more terrorism from the Middle East. As A.J. Muste said, "There is no way to peace; peace is the way." Let the inspections work.

Address to the Saginaw City Council
by Marc Beaudin

I would like to address the criticism that it isn't the place of the City of Saginaw to pass an anti-war resolution. Some say that Saginaw should only focus on its own problems and leave national and international affairs for others to worry about. They say, "Who do you think you are to take a stand on this issue? You're not Washington DC. Local government should limit itself to local issues and let the federal government do its job."

But I would like to remind those people that we are the federal government. This country is supposed to be a democracy, which means the people, all the people, are the government. Regular people from small cities and towns. The president, the Congress, the Senate, are merely our representatives, our servants. And the way this works is that it begins on the local level. It's our job as citizens to be political.

Some people make history, most are made by it. But history is made merely by those who choose to make it. Those who seize the opportunity to do right when it arises can help make a history to be proud of. This is one of those opportunities. Saginaw has the chance to take a stand for a peaceful resolution with Iraq. To support alternatives to war that will truly help the people of the Middle East and truly alleviate the threat of terrorism at home, rather than create a climate of mass-murder, instability, and vengeance.

We are faced with the opportunity to stand with hundreds of other cities and do what we know in our hearts is right. It's true that we're not Washington DC. But we are America, and we know right from wrong. And tonight, we have the chance to prove it.

Please, have the courage to make history.

An Instrument of Hate and Violence
by William P. Stone

I am no longer the silent majority. I am against the war.

I enjoy and expect the protection of my county. However, it is unclear to me the direct threat posed by Iraq. If the argument is "harboring those responsible for September 11th," then why not attack Pakistan? Is not that the likely hiding place of Osama bin Laden? Colin Powell believes it is.

In a recent *Newsweek* article, President Bush was quoted as saying that part of the US's intention is to free the Iraqi people--free them to worship as they please. I believe firmly in God and I believe, strongly, that our nation should not promote religion. Therefore, we don't have the right or Constitutional authority to "free" people so that they can worship God.

That's not our pluralistic country. And that may lead many people to conclude that our intent is theistic overthrow.

More and more people are beginning to see that North Korea posses a real and credible threat. The North Koreans have openly said they have nuclear warheads and the means to deliver them to US shores. Furthermore, two of our principle trading partners (Japan and South Korea) are easily within the immediate sphere of North Korea.

Finally, the US is setting a precedent that, like Pandora's Box, will forever unleash an evil once contained. For instance: Will China, thinking the people of Taiwan need to be free of their government, have the right to invade and overthrow that government? Or will the hatred of the US prompt more attacks against the US?

We are treading into a territory that may make history. And, it's not the legacy I wish to leave for my children and their children.

We need to be clear; hate isn't solved by hate. And, killing, as exemplified by Israel/Palestine, does not stop killing. The US needs to be a leader! We must be a force for good rather than an instrument of hate and violence in this world.

Take to the Streets
by Leo R. Lynch

Our political atmosphere reeks with the stench of White House hypocrisy and deception. While President Bush even within recent weeks has declared hat he had no immediate plans to use force in removing Saddam Hussein, there is ample evidence of a buildup of forces in the areas surrounding Iraq, particularly in the United States military base in Qatar.

While the Bush administration beats the drum for military action against Iraq, they would have us forget the history of our relationship with Iraq over the past two decades when the United States turned a blind eye to Iraq's use of chemical weapons. The United States provided covert help to Iraq in its 1980-1988 war with Iran, despite US knowledge that Iraq was using chemical weapons. Col. Walter P. Lang, now retired but a senior defense intelligence officer at the time covert assistance was given, is quoted as saying: "the use of gas on the battlefield was not a matter of deep strategic concern."

Secretary of Defense Donald Rumsfeld, who along with Vice President Cheney is among the president's biggest supporters of a military attack on Iraq, played a key role in President Reagan's efforts toward resumption of diplomatic relations between the US and Iraq. As Reagan's envoy to the Middle East, Rumsfeld met with Hussein in December 1983. On March 24, 1984, Rumsfeld went to Baghdad for meetings with then Iraqi Foreign Minister Tariq Aziz. That same day, United Press International issued a report from the United Nations that Iraq was using mustard gas containing a nerve agent against Iranian soldiers. Our State Department earlier that month has issued a similar report indicating that Iraq was using lethal chemical weapons. There is no record of a Rumsfeld statement on Iraq's use of poison gas until the Iraqi invasion of Kuwait in 1990. Bush's claim to the moral high ground on this issue rings hollow in light of these facts.

This matter serves to highlight a most disturbing characteristic of the Bush administration; namely, a hubris and arrogance that disdains to listen to alternative points of view, with a marked tendency to brand as unpatriotic those who would disagree with them. Bush would be well advised to listen to other voices, especially distinguished members of his own party who have expressed deep concern about his plans. Among them are former National Security Adviser Brent Scowcroft, former Secretary of State James Baker and US special Mideast envoy retired Marine General Anthony Zinni.

It is time for us to take our country back. It is time for us to demand that our government live up to the traditional standards of honorable international behavior. It is time for us, as responsible citizens, to demand of our president and the Congress clear and convincing arguments that a preemptive and unilateral attack on another sovereign state is morally defensible. Failing that, we must again take to the streets in protest of a government that, from all appearances, has lost its moral and ethical compass.

Vigilance in the Midst of Death:

The War Begins

3 AM in Baghdad
by Marc Beaudin

It's 3 am in Baghdad,
"City of Peace" according to
Arabian Nights,
those stories that lulled me to sleep,
to soft dreams.
How did we lose our childhood enchantment
with this far-off place
of silks and spices?
And yes, it's true:
the rivers we will soon send gunboats up–
will make to run red with the blood
of children–
are *those* rivers; the Tigris and the Euphrates,
that flowed from the Garden of Eden.
Have we forgotten that too?

It's 3 am in Baghdad
and I'm drinking water that once,
in the geologic measure of things,
carried holy fish from Eden to Mother Sea
I can taste the tears of Eve,
her black eyes reflecting the death-planes
vomiting out their bombs
while the men at the controls
imagine that she is their cold, blue-eyed mother;
they imagine that God doesn't hate them for their murder

It's 3 am in Baghdad
and I want to listen to a Miles Davis cd
but I'm afraid to turn off the radio
I'm sorry I ever paid my taxes
I'm burning a candle in my window
wondering if my neighbors can see it
over the glow of their television sets.
In the middle of *Kind of Blue*
one can imagine a world where blood
runs through the veins of children rather than rivers;
where oil is kept in the drum of the earth
cradling the bones of our ancestors

and the memories of stars

And now, it's 4 am in Baghdad:
the deadline of our appointed sociopath
the winds have calmed and the sands
have settled, revealing
the braided strands of stars
silently twisting across the darkness.
Eyes that haven't slept this night,
that haven't slept well in years,
look up at that luminous river,
mirror of the Biblical trickle below,
and see the coming storm,
the cleansing rain of fire,
"liberation" from the barrel of a gun.

I hold the water glass to my lips,
knowing that it is made of sands
that once blew across this desert
by winds that held the incense of Arabian nights.
Through its lens I see the
distorted image of a candle burning low,
and its reflection winking back at me from the glass
of the window; also made of these desert sands
and I wonder, how can we ever explain this
to our children?
How can we read them bedtime stories
that speak of a land that
we have destroyed?

It's 5 am in Baghdad,
city of peace,
the sun should be rising soon
but the night ahead of us is long.
I'll take a chance and put in Miles–
track 4–
pour another glass of water
and pray to what I no longer believe in.

To a Friend Who Supports the War
by Lisa Purchase Gould

Under vastly different circumstances I might offer some shred of support for this military action ... I agree that Hussein is probably a threat to international stability and a tyrant to the people of his own country. I also concede that diplomacy does not always work–sometimes force may be necessary to contain or overthrow an oppressive government. IF we could go in and handle this the right way, make a clean surgical strike and simply excise the troublesome individuals who appear to be at the root of the problem, then maybe this military action would be the best answer. IF we could quickly and efficiently rid Iraq of Hussein's oppression, with little civilian casualty, without destroying the country's infrastructure, without fating thousands of Iraqis to become homeless and penniless refugees, and without allowing chaos to follow in our wake as the government dissolves into tribalism and fractured political factions seeking control ... IF we could accomplish these things our "peace-keeping" mission might be warranted. I could support the idea of our involvement in such a high-minded endeavor. Unfortunately, I think this is a fictional scenario ... there is **no** chance that we will be able to accomplish these goals in a timely and efficient fashion, and the cost to all parties will be disproportionate to any benefits to be gained. We have a recent history of botched interventions, and the attention of the world is upon us to see if we can pull off what we have promised. We have pressed forward, against the advice of allied governments and a world of respected citizens, and set ourselves up for an impossible task.

Already we have found the citizens of Iraq less eager to welcome our presence than we thought. The soldiers have not thrown down their weapons and fled to our protection. Many of the citizens cower before our advance in much the same way that they have cowered before their former leader. And while I concede that some are merely afraid to act against their government in a time of uncertainty, and that they are heavily propagandized to hate and fear us, it does seem that the Iraqis may be somewhat reluctant to relinquish their oppressor to us. There is some merit to the idea "the devil we know is better than the devil we do not know." When we oust the powers that be, we will open a void to be filled with new and unknown evils. The inevitable chaos and uncertainty of the ensuing transition period may very well be followed by even *more* tyranny and oppression, and the people of Iraq may be left worse off than before we "rescued" them. Who will become the next dictator, and who gets to decide?

We do. We will stay and help the Iraqi people install a new, more democratic, more Western government. Our overthrow of their (admittedly oppressive) government smacks of Manifest Destiny and the Great White Hope, taking on religious and racial overtones ... *our God wants us to save these poor dark-eyed people from themselves and introduce them to our more modern and civilized way of government– they'll be better off that way.* We seem determined to repeat and repeat our own mistakes. We will attempt to replace Saddam with a leader who is sympathetic to our government, of course ... we will place our toady at the helm, in the same way that we helped the Shah to power in Iran–and then who will be our next Ayatollah? Any leader we install will be opposed by forces within Iraq, and as soon as we turn our attention elsewhere this new government will be subject to overthrow again, by a backlash of anti-American militants. Saddam himself is a product of our interventions in the Arab world, and we are not likely to fare much better on our next attempt to secure friends in the region.

We have raised the ire of all Arab nations by treading on their right to sovereignty. While Arab governments are officially urging their citizens to contain their protests to peaceful demonstration and not to take action against US citizens, we all know that we are virtually defenseless against militant groups or motivated individuals armed with box-cutters and a good case of small pox. And in case any were lacking motivation, a commentator pointed out on the radio today after watching television coverage of the invasion of Iraq: "Pictures of American soldiers killing Arabs ... Osama bin Laden could not have hoped for a more effective campaign to rally the Arab world."

It appears that many Americans believe that we are invading Iraq in retaliation for the terrorist attacks on September 11th. Even those who are against the war tend to make that erroneous connection ... "We've already killed more people over there than were killed here on 9/11." In reality, the two issues are separate and only tangentially related (if at all), but our fear of terrorism has given many of us the means to justify this war. It comes out sounding something like, "We've got to get them before they get us." This is faulty reasoning we would not accept from children on a playground, but it seems to have become our government's official policy on foreign affairs. This is a knee-jerk reaction: Arab = Terrorist, therefore we've got to strike first and make our country safe from these people. But striking first does not make us right, nor does it make us safe.

No matter how suspicious we may be of their intentions, we have to let the other party initiate any aggression. We can't just go in and attack any potential threat, based on suspicion and ideological differences ... if we are willing to invade a country, bomb its people, and overthrow its government, how then are we any different from terrorists (except that we have a lot more expensive weapons)? We don't get to wear the white hat when we strike first–now we're all down on the same level, and it gets pretty hard to distinguish the good guys from the bad guys.

And whatever the rhetoric about "freeing the people of Iraq," I doubt our government's motives are entirely altruistic. There is tyranny and oppression all over the world, and some other governments pose more of a threat to world peace, but when there is **oil** involved we feel the need to step up and intervene. This is a legitimate concern for our government ... the current administration is facing a shrinking economy, rising prices and unemployment, and declining popularity. An interruption in our oil supply would be devastating for our leaders' image ... we need oil to run our SUVs and televisions and Disneyland, to manufacture our cosmetics and to import our T-shirts ... without enough oil, there would be no CNN. A drastic cut in our oil supply would affect our lives and our economy, and no president wants to get stuck with that.

Bad economics are extremely unpopular (and boring on the news). War, on the other hand, is fairly popular (and exciting on the news). It unites us by giving us a common enemy. It distracts us from our petty grievances and inspires us to a patriotic spirit of sacrifice. It helps us feel strong and proud and gives us a "higher purpose." And it seems not to matter whether it's fact or fiction that leads us there, as long as we can tell ourselves the right story to justify our actions, war is good ... it's good news, it's good patriotism, it's good politics. It seems to be encoded into our DNA as humans, and we've only evolved from "conquering" people (now politically incorrect) to "liberating" them (the feel-good version of killing people) ... it's still about power, about getting to decide who lives and who dies; it's still about being right.

I don't presume to think that I have the answers, nor do I presume to finger-point and say that others' opinions are wrong. Maybe Hussein is enough of a threat to the world that something needed to be done. But I have a hard time accepting that *this* was the best or only option. Those who support the war can drag up quotes and evidence to support this course of action, but evidence can be found to support almost *any* viewpoint–the devil can quote the Bible to his own purposes. None of us have direct access to all the facts and all the nuances of this situation, so we each have to sift through the information that is available to us and form our own opinion based on what we can piece together. It all depends on who you trust enough to buy your advice and opinions from. CNN, with their up-close-and-personal coverage from their deeply embedded reporters? While this seems like a good idea, this coverage is far from complete and there is danger in thinking we are getting the whole story from these people. They have necessarily sold any shred of journalistic integrity in order to ride along to the front lines, and in return they are voluntarily under the thumb of the military ... they can't bad-mouth them; it's their ticket to the show and their ride home. In that sense, the reporters currently work for the military, providing us with only the information our government wants us to hear. When the war is over, tell-all books will come flying out of the woodwork as these reporters race to fill in the rest of the story, but for now our information is extremely restricted, and paints a seemingly detailed but grossly incomplete and inaccurate picture.

Atrocities are being committed in your name, in my name, as Americans, and I for one do not approve. Based on the slim evidence set before us, I do not wish to kill Iraqi people. I do not wish to take away their homes or their livelihood or their drinking water. I do not wish to answer to any Iraqi citizen who has lost their child, their brother, their parent to American bombs ... I would have no answer, no reason good enough to justify such loss–would anyone? It is too high a price to pay for such a dubious outcome, and it will not bring them or us peace or safety.

Since they are there and we are all wedded to this course of action for the time being, I would hope that our military personnel will act with grace and dignity, with honor and restraint, not with the hatred, fear, and machismo that will cause more damage and suffering for Iraqis and Americans alike. I respect their devotion to duty and their willingness to risk all, even though I can't support the administration that would give the orders to put them in this conflict. The world's gaze is upon these soldiers as our representatives, and I hope they somehow manage to act in a manner which does not make us out to be the demons that many now perceive. I wish them safety and compassion, and speedy return home. Already though, these hopes seem less and less likely to be fulfilled as time passes and their engagement there grows more destructive and complicated.

After various showdowns and military posturing, we have had to make an uneasy truce with Russia, China, and other world powers with inconveniently diverse cultural and ideological systems. Like wary animals that prowl the same territory, the greater beasts have learned to read the signs and respect the boundaries. It may be time to recognize the Arab world as another power, another beast that roams the world as an equal. Our foreign policy has long antagonized that particular beast, but it has found the fangs to fight for it's territory and there is nothing to be gained by trying to tame it now. This beast will not be caged or brought to heel, and we can no longer hope to control or tame it. We may prevail in this outright military confrontation, but this beast has far-reaching limbs which, hydra-like, will multiply each time we strike at it ... we will take down Hussein, but our methods will only serve to bring out new enemies, new fangs. As we seek to crush it, it will venomously bite at our heel and we will go down with it. We've got to learn a new way of dealing with it ... one that doesn't involve stepping on it.

We simplistically try to convince ourselves that we are crusaders against an Evil Dictator, but we cannot prevail against Evil in this way–it does not reside so conveniently in such a small and visible target. In the long run, this war is not a realistic or viable option, and with it we have compromised our own ideals, lost much of our government's credibility and clout in the international community, and further diminished our own security. We will eventually win the war, but we will *not* win the peace we pretend will follow it.

Add my small voice, reluctantly, to the growing voice of protest.

A Day in the Life of War

(for my kids: Dylan & Danessa, Cameron & Terra, for Lupe & Lorde, Julianna, Ethan, Parker, Ryan and all of them everywhere – March 21, 2003)

by Al Hellus

Kids live here
in safety
and reasonable freedom.
They are well loved
and fed
and a little bit
off the wall.

This is a good thing.

There is war out there
and fog
and various
forms of pestilence,
but here:
there are kids
who draw
and make volcanos
and laugh
their asses off
and have to go
to school
soon.

The uncle
sits at the
kitchen table
at 6:30
in the morning
and tears
escape
from his eyes
as he hears
them sleeping –
comprehends
the hugeness of
it.

Bombs drop,
tanks scurry
across the desert
sands
and they talk
talk talk talk
about it
on the
television.

Dogs,
large and small,
yawn, stretch,
go back to sleep.

The uncle is
sleepy himself,
but a damn
lucky man.

He knows this,
takes a sip
of his
cooling coffee,

as birds awake
to continue
their endless
conversations.

Helping Iraq Kill with Chemical Weapons:
The Relevance of Yesterday's US Hypocrisies Today
by Dr. Elson E. Boles

You may feel disgusted by the hypocrisy of US plans to make war on Iraq and sickened at the inevitable slaughter of thousands of people. But if you can only vaguely recall the details of how deep the hypocrisy goes, then read on.

The US not only helped arm Iraq with military equipment right up to the time of the Kuwait invasion in 1989, as did Germany, Britain, France, Russia and others, and the US not only sold Iraq chemical materials for their war against Iran between 1985-1988, but the US also helped Iraq gas and kill tens of thousands of Iranians. As summed up in the *New York Times* (10-11-02) by reporter Nicholas Kristof, "In the 1980's we provided his army with satellite intelligence so that it could use chemical weapons against Iranian soldiers. When Saddam used nerve gas and mustard gas against Kurds in 1988, the Reagan administration initially tried to blame Iran. We shipped seven strains of anthrax to Iraq between 1978 and 1988."

According to another *New York Times* article (8-29-02) Col. Walter P. Lang, a senior defense intelligence officer at the time, explained that DIA and CIA officials "were desperate to make sure that Iraq did not lose [to Iran.] ... The use of gas on the battlefield by the Iraqis was not a matter of deep strategic concern," he said. One veteran said that the Pentagon "wasn't so horrified by Iraq's use of gas. ... It was just another way of killing people, whether with a bullet or phosgene, it didn't make any difference."

Now consider how deceptive the recent comments from the White House are. In late September spokesman Ari Fleischer said that British Prime Minister Blair's dossier of evidence is "frightening in terms of Iraq's intentions and abilities to acquire weapons." A few days later, while making his case against Saddam, President Bush said "He's used poison gas on his own people." Bush deceives because he hides the fact that US officials, including his father, had no qualms about helping Saddam gas Iranians. What is truly frightening are the US policies toward Iraq, the cover ups of those policies, and the US officials who personally profit in the millions of dollars from those policies. To whatever degree Saddam is a tyrant, he would not be that without the US government. Thus, the question is not whether Saddam is willing to use chemical or other weapons of mass destruction again. The question is whether the US is willing to sell materials for weapons of mass destruction to dictators and is willing to help them kill thousands.

Recently disclosed details about Iraq killing Iranians with US-supplied chemical and biological materials and military targeting assistance significantly deepens our understanding of the current hypocrisy. It began with "Iraqgate"–when US policy makers, financiers, and arms manufacturers and suppliers made massive profits from sales to Iraq of myriad chemical, biological, and conventional weapons, as well as the equipment to make nuclear weapons. Reporter Russ Baker noted, for example, that, "on July 3, 1991, the Financial Times reported that a Florida company run by an Iraqi national had produced cyanide–some of which went to Iraq for use in chemical weapons--and had shipped it via a CIA contractor." This was just the tip of a mountain of scandals.

A major break in uncovering the Iraqgate scandals began with a riveting 1992 *Nightline* episode which revealed that top officials of the Reagan administration, the State Department, the Pentagon, CIA, and DIA, collectively engaged in a massive cover-up of the USS Vincennes' whereabouts and actions when it shot down an Iranian airliner in 1988 killing over 200 civilians. The "massive cover-up" Koppel explained, was designed to hide the US secret war against Iran, in which, among other actions, US Special Operations troops and Navy SEALS sunk half of Iran's navy while giving battle plans and logistical information to Iraqi ground forces in a coordinated offensive.

In continuing the probe, as Koppel explained in 1992, "It is becoming increasingly clear that George Bush [Sr.], operating largely behind the scenes throughout the 1980s, initiated and supported much of the financing, intelligence, and military help that built Saddam's Iraq into the aggressive power that the United States ultimately had to destroy."

A PBS *Frontline* episode, "The Arming of Iraq" (1990) detailed much of the conventional and so-called "dual-use" equipment sold to Iraq. The public learned from other sources that at least since the mid-1980s, the US was selling chemical and biological material for weapons to Iraq and orchestrating private sales. These sales began soon after current Secretary of Defense Donald Rumsfeld traveled to Baghdad in 1983 and 1984 and met with Saddam Hussein on behalf of the Reagan administration. In the last major battle of the Iran-Iraq war, some 65,000 Iranians were killed, many by gas with chemicals and technology imported from the US and its allies.

Investigators turned up new scandals, including the involvement of *Banca Nazionale del Lavoro* (BNL), the giant Italian bank, and many of the very same circles of arms suppliers, covert operators, and policy makers in and out of the US government and active in those roles for years. The National Security Council, CIA and other US agencies tacitly approved about $4 billion in unreported loans to Iraq through the giant Italian bank's Atlanta branch. Iraq, with the blessing and official approval of the US government, purchased computer controlled machine tools, computers, scientific instruments, special alloy steel and aluminum, chemicals, and other industrial goods for Iraq's missile, chemical, biological and nuclear weapons programs.

However, the early reports on BNL's activities and the startling revelations that the US government knew that BNL was financing billions of dollars of purchases illegally, were rather comical in view of later revelations regarding who was involved. US government officials didn't just know and approve, but some were employees at BNL directly or indirectly. It was Representative Henry Gonzalez (D-Texas) who relentlessly brought key information into the Congressional Record (despite stern warnings by the State Department to stop his personal investigation for the sake of "national security").

Gonzalez revealed, for example, that Brent Scowcroft served as Vice Chairman of Kissinger Associates until being appointed as National Security Advisor to President Bush in January 1989. As Gonzalez reported, "Until October 4,1990, Mr. Scowcroft owned stock in approximately 40 US corporations, many of which were doing business in Iraq." Scowcroft's stock included that in Halliburton Oil, also doing business in Iraq at the time, which had also been run by current Vice President Dick Cheney for a time. Recall that this year President George Bush Sr. faced suspicion of insider trading in relation to selling his stock in Halliburton. The companies that Scowcroft owned stock in, according to Gonzalez, "received more than one out of every eight US export licenses for exports to Iraq. Several of the companies were also clients of Kissinger Associates while Mr. Scowcroft was Vice Chairman of that firm." Thus, Kissinger Associates helped US companies obtain US export licenses with BNL-finance so Iraq could purchase US weapons and materials for its weapons programs.

Many US businessmen and officials made handsome profits. This included Henry Kissinger, the former Secretary of State under Richard Nixon, who was an employee of BNL while BNL was simultaneously a paying client of Kissinger Associates. Gonzalez reported that Mr. Alan Stoga, a Kissinger Associates executive, met Saddam Hussein in Baghdad in June 1989. "Many Kissinger Associates clients received US export licenses for exports to Iraq. Several were also the beneficiaries of BNL loans to Iraq," said Mr. Gonzalez. Kissinger admitted that "it is possible that somebody may have advised a client on how to get a license."

Perhaps the most bizarre revelations about the involvement of former US officials concerned a Washington-based enterprise called "Global Research" which played a middleman role in selling uniforms to Iraq. It was run by none other than Spiro Agnew (Nixon's former VP who resigned to avoid bribery and tax evasion charges), John Mitchell (Nixon's chief of staff and Watergate organizer), and Richard Nixon himself. In the mid-1980s, more than a decade after Watergate, Nixon wrote a cozy letter to former dictator and friend Nicolae Ceausescu to close the deal. Global Research, incidentally, swindled the Iraqis, who thought they were getting US-made uniforms for desert conditions. Instead they received, and discarded, winter uniforms from Romania.

By late 1992, the sales of chemical and biological weapons were revealed. Congressional Records of Senator Riegle's investigation of the Gulf War Syndrome show that the US government approved sales of large varieties of chemical and biological materials to Iraq. These included anthrax, components of mustard gas, botulinum toxins (which causes paralysis of the muscles involving swallowing and is often fatal), histoplasma capsulatum (which may cause pneumonia, enlargement of the liver and spleen, anemia, acute inflammatory skin disease marked by tender red nodules), and a host of other nasty chemical materials.

To top it all off, there is the question as to whether Iraq's invasion of Kuwait was a set up. Evidence indicates that the US knew of Iraq's plans–after all, the military and intelligence agencies of the two countries were working very closely. Newspaper reports about the infamous meeting between then-Ambassador Glaspie and Iraqi officials, and a special ABC report in the series "A Line in the Sand," both indicated that, although the US officials told Iraq that it disapproved, they indicated that the US would not interfere.

Bear in mind the attitude of the US policy makers not only regarding Iraq's use of gas against Iranians, but in general. Richard Armitage, then Assistant Secretary of Defense for International Security Affairs and now Deputy Secretary of State, said with a hint of pride in his voice that the US "was playing one wolf off another wolf" in pursuing our so-called national interest. This kind of cool machismo resembled the pride that Oliver North verbalized with a grin during the Iran-Contra hearings as "a right idea" with regard to using the Ayatollah's money to fund the Contras. The setting up of Iraq thus would be very consistent with the goals and the character of US foreign policy in the Middle East: to control the region's states either for US oil companies or as bargaining chips in deals with other strong countries, and to profit by selling massive quantities of weapons to states that will war with or deter those states that oppose US "interests."

The problem that Armitage refers to was the fact that by 1990, the US and allied arming of Iraq had given Iraq a decisive military edge over Iran, which upset the regional "balance." The thinking among the US hawks was Iraq's military needed to somehow be returned to its 1980 level. An invasion of Kuwait would enable the US to do that.

But initially many arms suppliers opposed the war on Iraq because they had been making huge profits from arms sales to Saddam's regime during the 1980s. Indeed, one US official interviewed expressed his disappointment with Iraq's invasion and the subsequent Gulf War because the relationship with Iraq could have continued to be "very profit...uh mutually profitable."

Bush Sr. and others expected that after the war, Saddam would capitulate to US designs on the region. With a heeled Saddam, the interests of arms suppliers, defense contractors, and the many US oil corporations could be renewed. Iraq would have to re-arm itself and invest in oil drilling and processing facilities that were destroyed by US forces. And to pay for all that, Iraq would have to sell oil cheap, which served the interests both of the giant oil corporations and the American public who had begun buying GM SUVs en masse. It would be good for US business.

The invasion today is, above all, to renew the US's firm access to Iraqi oil. As reported recently in the *New York Times*, former CIA director R. James Woolsey, who has been one of the leading advocates of forcing Hussein from power, argues that, "It's pretty straightforward, France and Russia have oil companies and interests in Iraq. They should be told that if they are of assistance in moving Iraq toward decent government, we'll do the best we can to ensure that the new government and American companies work closely with them. If they throw in their lot with Saddam, it will be difficult to the point of impossible to persuade the new Iraqi government to work with them."

His views are of course supported by the new Iraqi government-in-waiting. Faisal Qaragholi, the petroleum engineer who directs the London office of the Iraqi National Congress (INC), an umbrella organization of opposition groups that is backed by the United States, says that, "Our oil policies should be decided by a government in Iraq elected by the people." Ahmed Chalabi, the INC leader, put it more bluntly and said that he favored a US-led consortium to develop Iraq's oil fields, which would replace the existing agreements that Iraq has with Russia and France. "American companies will have a big shot at Iraqi oil," Chalabi said.

Note also that Bush and company have a personal stake in unilateral action. According to Leroy Sievers and the *Nightline* staff at ABC, "Dick Cheney's Halliburton Co. had interests in Iraqi oil production after the [Gulf] war." *New York Times* reporter Nicholas Kristof further explained, "But when Mr. Cheney was running Halliburton, the oil services firm, it sold more equipment to Iraq than any other company did. As first reported by *The Financial Times* on Nov. 3, 2000, Halliburton subsidiaries submitted $23.8 million worth of contracts with Iraq to the United Nations in 1998 and 1999 for approval by its sanctions committee."

Following the Gulf War, Cheney, Bush Sr. and others didn't expect that Saddam would refuse to abide by US interests and join the so-called "family of nations." This is really what President Bush Jr. meant when he said at a cabinet meeting on September 24, 2002 that he intends "to hold Saddam Hussein to account for a decade of defiance"--that is, he has defied their ability to make huge profits from arms sales to Iraq and from developing Iraq's oil fields.

There is no shock about any of this, nor about the sordid assortment of officials and individuals directly or indirectly involved– from the infamous US-based international arms dealer Sarkis Songhanalian and former General Secord, to Oliver North and Richard Nixon–and many others. They had been part of covert US arms and drug deals dating back decades. Iraqgate was in fact also part of Irangate, and both are about a shadow government that circumvents domestic and international laws in arming regimes and terrorist organizations to enhance the profits of US businessmen and corporations.

The public learned since the mid-1980s that the shadow government folks played all sides of various wars, and made curious business alliances. Profits were good, but there were also ideological reasons. While arming Iraq and putting proceeds into their pockets, the covert operators also armed Iran. Israel of course, had also been arming Iran since the Ayatollah came into power in order to counter Iraq. The US soon joined these operations after Reagan came to power.

Oliver North, Bush Sr., Dennis McFarlane, and General Secord, and others purchased from the CIA spare parts for US-made weapons and more than two thousand TOW missiles, which the CIA had purchased at discount rates from the Pentagon. Secord and North sold the weapons and parts to Iran in exchange for cash and the release of US hostages in Lebanon.

In public, Ronnie Reagan repeatedly condemned negotiations with terrorists in principle and even stated on national TV that there had been no negotiations with terrorists. He went back on air a few months later and said that while he still didn't believe "in his heart" that the US had negotiated with terrorists, the facts told him "otherwise." He escaped impeachment because he "couldn't remember" signing detailed instructions for sales of weapons to Iran and for the diversion of money to the Contras.

Insiders considered these trades "business as usual." Retired General Secord, for instance, unashamedly told Congressional investigators during the Iran-Contra hearings that his arms-dealing firm, the "Enterprise," which sold the TOWs to other brokers and then to Iran, was a legitimate profit-making business. And as we all know, at the other end of the deal, North channeled a portion of the proceeds from those sales through Swiss banks and to the terrorist Contras [based] in Honduras. Their job was to overthrow the Sandinista regime [in Nicaragua] that overthrew the brutal 43-year Somoza family dictatorship supported by the US.

Again, in legal terms, the scandal was not only that Reagan's administration circumvented the Boland Amendment which outlawed military support to the Contras, but also that the CIA had mined the harbors of Nicaragua. When the US was taken to the International Court of Justice (ICJ) and convicted of violating international laws, President Reagan disregarded this conviction saying the ICJ had no jurisdiction over the United States.

Bush Jr. has stated the following reasons for invading Iraq, all of which are accurate except the last: (1) Iraq used chemical weapons, (2) Iraq tried to build nuclear weapons, and (3) the US tried to bring Iraq into the "family of nations" (said first by Bush Sr). He is correct that Iraq was willing to use chemical weapons and has been trying to build nuclear weapons for years. Of course, he just fails to mention that the US was willing to sell, and to help Iraq use, chemical weapons of mass destruction and that his friends profited handsomely in so doing. He also fails to note that today Hussein is not seen as an immediate threat by his Arab neighbors, none of whom have called for his ouster, and that Iraq has only a shadow of the power it had in 1990. There is no evidence to support Bush or Blair's claims that Iraq still has and is preparing to use chemical or biological weapons.

Lastly, what about Bush Jr.'s third contention, that the US had tried to bring Saddam into the "family of nations?" In view of the thousands upon thousands of women, children, and men butchered with US battle plans and arms, as well as arms from Europe, one could only characterize that family as being composed of unscrupulous, profiteering, vile accomplices to mass murder. Perhaps this is also a reason why the Bush administration opposes the formation of the World Court and has made US politicians and military personnel exempt from its jurisdiction and international law.

War is Unacceptable
by Dr. Scott M. Youngstedt

War is unacceptable.
War is a horror.
War is an abomination.

People die in war. It is quite possible that hundreds of thousands of people will die in this war. It is also quite possible, as has been the overall trend in wars since World War I, that the majority of them will be civilians. (I also don't want soldiers to die, neither US nor Iraqi.)

I support US soldiers, therefore I support sending them home to their families. I support sending them to do courageous work like removing land mines in Vietnam, Angola, Afghanistan, Rwanda, and Nicaragua, which directly promotes human security and liberty.

During the recent war in Afghanistan, 3,000 civilians were killed. This was calculated by Marc Herold, a professor of Economics at the University of New Hampshire (now corroborated by many other analysts), primarily drawing from scattered stories buried within the pages of mainstream newspapers and news agencies such as the *New York Times*, *Washington Post*, *The Times* of London, Reuters, et al. Unless and until we can feel as much compassion and sadness for these Afghanis as we do for those who died on 9-11, we will find it difficult to avoid war.

WAR IS TERRORISM

I don't mean this literally, it is important to recognize their differences. But here's my point: Millions of Iraqi husbands, wives, daughters, sons, carpenters, beggars, electricians, farmers, potters, butchers, professors, students, and traders are being thoroughly terrorized as I speak. Their terror is not qualitatively different from the terror we felt on 9-11. War and terrorism are primarily about one thing: killing people. Never accept the euphemism "collateral damage"–they are human beings.

WAR IS UNACCEPTABLE

If it is possible to speak of degrees of unacceptability, then this war is particularly unacceptable. There were many reasonable diplomatic and legal opportunities to avoid this illegal war. (That's right, according to established principles of international law this is an illegal war. Though I must say it is also disheartening that we *have* an international concept of "legal war.")

The vast majority of the people of the world, the majority of the members of the UN Security Council, and the majority of the five permanent members of the Council are opposed to this war.

As many experts around the world argue, it is neither clear that the Iraqi regime is a threat to its neighbors, let alone the US, nor is it clear that they possess WMDs. With respect to the latter, (1) Scott Ritter, former chief inspector of weapons after the Gulf War has publicly stated that inspections were enormously successful in locating and destroying at least 95% of Iraq's WMDs, and (2) for the past three months or so the most advanced weapons inspection team ever assembled (using US intelligence) has found virtually nothing, only the al-Samoud missiles (which have, I believe, a range of about 110 km or about 20 km more than allowed) which the Iraqis agreed to destroy. Granted, Iraq is a big country and it is possible that they are hiding WMDs. Weapons inspectors should be given time to do their jobs properly and in accordance with international law.

Unfortunately, this war reflects the overall direction of the Bush administration, an administration which has shown complete disregard for international cooperation and international law—

- by pulling the US out of the Kyoto Treaty on the environment,
- by withdrawing from missile treaties with Russia,
- by refusing to support the International Court of Justice,
- by clumsily and needlessly alienating many of the United States' closest allies,
- by seeking to undermine the credibility of the UN with respect to Iraq.

Furthermore, Bush's new doctrine of "preemptive strike," which allows for the use of nuclear weapons, sets a particularly dangerous and chilling precedent. Even more, it has already made the world more dangerous, unstable, and prone to war. By the same logic, why can't other nations carry out "preemptive strikes," with their own nukes, against foes who might strike them later?

And beware, "preemptive strike" is a euphemism for "first strike with overwhelming force preferably against an already severely weakened adversary."

HYPOCRISY

This war also involves layers of hypocrisy and lies. Manuel Noriega, Osama bin Laden, and Saddam Hussein were all once close allies of the US.

US corporations, sanctioned by the US Department of Commerce, repeatedly sold chemical and biological weapons to Saddam Hussein in the 1980s. The US government provided battle plans to the Iraqis for deploying these weapons against Iran. A top government official simply said, "It's just another way of killing people."

The United States' new alliance with the Northern Alliance in Afghanistan fits the pattern of the recent history of US foreign policy. Many Afghanis at first welcomed the Taliban as a better alternative to the terrorism and destruction perpetrated by the Northern Alliance. Before, during, and since the US led war in Afghanistan, the Northern Alliance has murdered thousands of POWs. And now, despite repeated promises, the US has largely abandoned Afghanistan. Will Iraq be any different? Probably not, except for the fact that it has oil; the second largest known reserves in the world.

DISTRACTION FROM TERRORISM, INCREASED VULNERABILITY

Even though more than half of Americans now believe that Saddam Hussein was responsible for 9-11 according to a recent poll, there is no evidence of any links between Hussein and al Qaeda. The CIA has found none.

This war will only fuel anger around the world and serve to inspire future terrorists. People around the world, including the Muslim world, do not hate American people or American freedom, but many do hate our policies. (This point was forcefully made by all of the world's leading scholars on the Middle East who visited SVSU for our Middle East Symposium last fall.)

I spent a month earlier this year in Niger, a Muslim country. Nigerians love Americans and admire our freedoms. They were enormously saddened by 9-11. They agreed that this was not a jihad. They agreed that the highjackers committed suicide–a grave sin. They agreed that terrorism is unacceptable. (Similar views were expressed in Morocco and Tunisia where I recently spent time as a Fulbright scholar.)

Attacking the World Trade Center was no more a Muslim act, than the current bombing of Baghdad is a Christian or Jewish act. Both are unacceptable to these three faiths. But while people in Niger do not agree with al Qaeda's tactics, the words of Osama bin Laden do resonate with many people.

Bin Laden is angry about the huge US military presence in Saudi Arabia, the holiest land in Islam. He is angry about the US support of Israel's oppression of the Palestinians. (I might add that Israel and the US are blatantly violating many UN Security Council resolutions.) He is angry about the sanctions against Iraq which have led to enormous suffering among Iraqis. He is angry about the US support for brutal, anti-Islamic dictatorships.

None of this in any way justifies terrorism, even though his anger is very understandable. Unfortunately, Osama bin Laden was hoping for this war as he knows it will help him recruit more terrorists.

PEACE IS NOT APPEASING HUSSEIN

Imposing severe economic sanctions, imposing weapons inspections teams with virtually unfettered access, imposing unilaterally declared "no-fly zones" (these are not sanctioned by the UN) is not appeasement.

PEACE IS GOOD FOR CHILDREN AND ALL LIVING THINGS

In what kind of world do we want our children and their children to live? We teach them not to fight. What does war teach them about fighting?

PEACE IS PATRIOTIC

Peace is patriotic before war.
Peace is patriotic during war.
Peace is patriotic after war.

In a democratic society citizens have not only the right but the responsibility to freely express their views. We must never relinquish these rights and responsibilities. We must never accept erosion of our civil liberties and Constitutional rights in the name of war.

FINALLY ... WAR IS UNACCEPTABLE

War is unacceptable for the 21st century if we are to survive and evolve as a civilized species.

Monday, President Bush spoke of a "moment of truth." I believe it was a moment of truth, but my conclusions are very different from his. This was the moment when Bush could have chosen peace and could have made strides toward proving his absurd claim that "we are a peaceful nation." He utterly failed and the world is now much worse off for it.

Despite the horror and sadness that I feel today, I envision a day when we human beings will reflect on war with absolute revulsion and find it impossible to believe that we could have been so barbaric. But the only way we will get there from here is if we continue to oppose war and promote peace.

Supporting the Troops: Myth vs. Reality
by Marc Beaudin

The anti-war movement has met with much criticism from various segments of the population, and the most often levied criticism is that by protesting the war, we are not supporting the troops. We see and hear it in editorials, letters to the editor, and yelled from passing SUV's at our vigils. We are told that "the time for protest is over, once the war starts we must be united" (as if democracy should only be used when it's irrelevant, but when the serious issues are at hand, we must let tyranny rule). We are told that we must support the troops because "they are fighting for our freedom," or "national security," or "Iraqi liberation," or even "to protect our right to protest" (as if Saddam were on his way over here to repeal our civil liberties–not that Ashcroft needs any help with that) ... or they are fighting for some other aim, so intrinsically good that it is beyond discussion, let alone doubt.

But I have doubts.

I have doubts about the legality of the war, and more than that, I have doubts that anyone who is in support of this war, and the current US administration, can honestly say that they are also in support of the troops.

Just what does it mean to "support the troops"? This administration and their media lap dogs seem to believe that support merely means to blindly encourage them to go off and blindly kill and die; whenever, wherever, and whoever they are told to.

But I have to believe that true support means something deeper than this. Certainly supporting the troops means making sure that they are cared for and protected as much as possible, and not just during a conflict when the media hails them as heroes and it's so easy to sit back here at home and wave a flag. No, true support means caring for their needs after they've "done their duty" as well.

So let's take a look at how the government scores on this count.

According to the Department of Veterans' Affairs, of nearly 700,000 vets from Desert Storm and Desert Shield (the video-game names for the mostly-unopposed massacre of the first Gulf War), more than 300,000 have sought VA health care and more than 200,000 have filed for disability. The shocking level of these numbers will be discussed below, but it's no surprise that with an already under-funded VA most vets wait 6 months to see a doctor and most wait 6 months to receive a decision on a VA disability claim. Imagine what that means: the suffering, the lost wages, the not knowing when or if help is possible; month after month.

Unfortunately, I think vets are going to soon look on that situation as the "good old days." Here's why: First, two weeks before the war, Bush cut 275 million dollars from the health care budget of the Department of Veterans' Affairs. Second, the day after the House voted to "support the troops and the president," they then voted to cut VA funding for 2004 by $463 million, and a ten-year reduction of $25 BILLION. These cuts are in the area of veterans' health benefits and disability benefits. They also raised the enrollment fee for VA health care to $250, added a deductible that can be up to $1,500, and doubled the co-pay for prescription drugs. But apparently this wasn't quite enough to show how much the House and the Bush administration support the troops, so they also cut $204 million from the Impact Aid Program that supports the education of children of soldiers.[1]

So much for caring for the troops when they return. Now what about protecting them while they're gone?

I mentioned before the very high numbers of disabled vets from the Gulf War. According to the non-partisan Gulf War Resource Center, 36% of Gulf War vets filed for disability and 29% were given disability status. This was in a war that basically had no enemy. The Iraqi military was totally under-supplied, out-numbered, and unsupervised. They surrendered in droves. The big fear was that Saddam would unleash his dreaded chemical weapons—he never did. So how on earth do we have 29% of our vets disabled? Well, 20% of that 29 are suffering from what's become known as Gulf War Syndrome.

Gulf War Syndrome is characterized by things like chronic pain, fatigue, wasting away of muscles, cancers (especially leukemia), lung and skin problems, cerebral lesions; and it is passed on to the new-born babies of those with the Syndrome in the form of deformities such as hydrocephalus (abnormal increase in cerebrospinal fluid in the cranial cavity which leads to an enlarged skull and atrophy of the brain), encephalitis (inflammation of the brain), spinal bifida (incomplete closure of the bones of the spinal column so spinal marrow is unprotected), monstrous limb deformities, and being born without a head or heart.

Now obviously, if you really support the troops, you would want to know what caused this and make sure it never happens again. However, the government (and not just the current administration, but Clinton and King George I, too) denies that it exists. "It's just stress, it's

---

[1] Press release from Congressman Ted Strickland (www.house.gov/ strickland/Budget2003Rel.html); www.uslaboragainstwar.org; www.winwithoutwar.org.

all in your head." As far as the cancers and deformities that can't be so easily ignored, they still refuse to take responsibility, to accept any studies done on it, or conduct the proper tests to specify where it came from.[1]

Well, there are several candidates for the cause of Gulf War Syndrome:

- Required vaccinations (some experimental and given without notice; again our soldiers become guinea pigs ... like in the nuclear radiation exposure tests of World War II and the LSD experiments of Vietnam),
- Pesticides,
- Bombardment of chemical plants, and
- Depleted uranium, which is used to make bullets ranging in size from 25 mm to 120 mm for use by US tanks, helicopters and planes because it's so dense that it easily rips through tank armor and concrete bunkers. It is also used as armor on our tanks. Depleted uranium, or DU, is radioactive waste from nuclear power plants.

Of all these possible causes, depleted uranium is the most likely culprit for two reasons: First, Gulf War Syndrome is also called NATO Syndrome because NATO troops who fought in Kosovo with US and British depleted uranium are suffering all the same symptoms. Second, Iraqi civilians, who did not receive vaccinations, pesticides, or bombard chemical plants are also suffering from this syndrome, and in much higher numbers. For example, according to Aws Albaiti, a physician working in Baghdad from 1990 to 1999, leukemia among Iraqi children rose 1200% after the first Gulf War.[2]

The Gulf War battlefield is littered with 300 tons of radioactive dust and shrapnel from 1991. Again, people will look at that as the good old days, because in the current war, we're still using depleted uranium (probably a lot more this time), still failing to inform soldiers of the risks and even denying that there even are risks.

So much for protecting the troops while in combat.

I mentioned earlier the issue of the legality of this war. Let's

---

[1] Michel Collon. "The 'NATO Syndrome' – Arms, Profits and Lies: Who Has Been Concealing the Dangers of Depleted Uranium for the Last Ten Years, and Why?" International Action Center, www.iacenter.org.

[2] Quoted in: Colligan, Paddy. "Campaign to Ban Weopons: Soldiers, Doctors Testify on Effects of DU." International Action Center, www.iacenter.org.

take a look at that, because surely, if you support the troops, you would seek to prevent them from committing war crimes.

The rules for soldiers are pretty clear on this. The International Military Tribunal at Nuremberg following WWII established the responsibility of soldiers to refuse to follow illegal orders. No longer could someone commit crimes and atrocities with the excuse that he or she was "just following orders." This is spelled out in the US Military Code of Conduct which requires soldiers to obey all legal orders and to disobey all illegal ones.

So is this war illegal; and therefore, obeying orders to fight it violate the Nuremberg Tribunal and the US Military Code of Conduct?

Well, I think it's clearly illegal beyond a doubt. Anyone honestly looking at it, any legal scholar who isn't being paid by the administration, would agree that it is. Why?

First of all, Article 2 of the United Nations Charter, Points 3 and 4 state: "All Members shall settle their international disputes by peaceful means in such a manner that international peace and security, and justice, are not endangered." "All Members shall refrain in their international relations from the threat or use of force against the territorial integrity or political independence of any state, or in any other manner inconsistent with the Purposes of the United Nations." The only uses of force authorized by the United Nations are when the Security Council decides that a "threat to the peace, breach of the peace, or act of aggression" has occurred (Article 39), and they have exhausted all diplomatic (Article 40) and non-military measures (Article 41), then they can decide to use force (Article 42). Article 51 provides for the use of force in self-defense (individual or collective) only *"if an armed attack occurs."*

The Bush administration tried to get around this legality problem in two ways.

They first tried to link Iraq with the September 11th attacks and therefore call this war an act of self-defense. This approach fails in a couple of ways: Self-defense means an immediate response to armed attack for the purpose of repulsing that attack until the United Nations can step in and resolve the situation; not invading a nation a year and a half after this supposed attack occurred. And, there simply is no evidence of Iraq in any way being connected with 9/11.

Donald Rumsfeld asked the CIA on 10 separate occasions to find a link. They couldn't, but they sure tried. The CIA speculated on supposed meetings between Iraqi officials and al Queda members, and supposed financing by Iraq of terrorist organizations, but has never produced any credible evidence.

The key piece of purported evidence is a meeting in Prague between an Iraqi official and Mohamed Atta, described as a "ringleader of the suicide hijackers." However, according to Czech police and intelligence, the Mohamed Atta who was visiting Prague (though not meeting with the Iraqi official) had a different identity card number, was the wrong age and the wrong nationality. The man who did meet with the Iraqi official was an Iraqi used car dealer from Germany. The real Mr. Atta, according to the FBI, was in Florida at the time. (Though they didn't say whether or not he was meeting with Jeb Bush).

The other tactic the Bush administration took to skirt the legality issue was to try to invoke UN Resolution 687. This resolution allowed the US and others to use necessary means to get Iraq out of Kuwait. The exact wording is "to uphold Resolution 660 [which is getting Iraq out of Kuwait] and relevant subsequent resolutions." Bush says this phrase "relevant subsequent resolutions" refers to Iraq's disarmament. However, 687 clearly states in its preamble which resolutions it is referring to: those between 660 and 687 that deal solely with the expulsion of Iraq from Kuwait.

The United States is bound by its Constitution to consider any ratified treaty as "the law of the land." The UN Charter was ratified by the US Congress in 1945. Therefore, even if we wanted to ignore the UN rules, we are still, by doing that, in violation of our own Constitution.

From all of this, it seems pretty clear to me that 1) the war is illegal, 2) soldiers are required to disobey illegal orders, 3) fighting an illegal war is failing to disobey an illegal order, and 4) supporting such action is wrong.

If you support the troops, rather than, or at least in addition to, criticizing the anti-war demonstrators and putting flags and yellow ribbons everywhere, I would suggest putting time and energy into demanding adequate funding for health benefits, a ban on depleted uranium so there is less of a need for these benefits, and the immediate return of the troops who are now committing war crimes in Iraq.

Support for Troops Lacking
by Mary Ellen Garrett

I am a member of Tri-City Action for Peace. You may have seen us standing vigil in front of the Courthouse, and a group of people who oppose us gathered across the street. They have signs that say "Support President Bush and our Troops."

They accuse us of not supporting the troops. I would like to clearly state that this is a fallacy. We do support the troops, but not the way these people mean. We are concerned for our troops' personal safety and well-being. We don't want them to die, be tortured, get cancer from depleted uranium used in weapons, or have to suffer the psychological damage that war inflicts. We want the Veterans Administration to take care of them when they return, and we would never spit on them or call them names.

I would like to address the question of who really supports the troops. The pro-war protesters signs saying "Support President Bush and our Troops" imply that the two go hand-in-hand. This makes no sense.

President Bush doesn't really seem to care about the troops. He pays a lot of lip service to them, but what s he really doing for them?

He sent them off to war to be poisoned, killed, injured, and at the very least, taken away from their families. He supports cutting millions in Veterans Administration spending when it is already seriously underfunded and understaffed. He threatened to veto a proposal for concurrent military and veteran benefits. He supports cutting education benefits for the children of military people.

The House Budget Committee is proposing a cut in veterans benefits by $15 billion over the next 10 years, starting next year with a cut of $463 million. The Veterans Administration now has 1.4 million more clients enrolled than in 1996 with 20,000 fewer employees. After the war, there will be at least 600,000 more veterans.

With all the talk of how much he appreciates the troops, Bush supports this proposal.

I would suggest that the supporters of Bush and those who say they support the troops start writing letters to the House Budget Committee and their beloved president instead of directing their anger at anti-war protesters.

We are praying for the safety of all people, including the troops.

Letter to TCAP

by Joseph M. Locke

Dear TCAP,

I, too, must say that I cannot support the troops and at the same time say I am against war. How could I say I support someone who's going off to slaughter the lives of innocent Iraqis? Yes, some people might think this is being disrespectful of "our men" or that I'm not being "patriotic." My response to this can only be that it's not that I don't love my country, but I love the world over. I will never let ego make me feel that I'm somehow better than someone else just because I live in the US. Some may say that dissent and peace are patriotic, but I will admit that, despite believing in both dissent and peace, I would never consider myself patriotic. The definition of patriotism is "love of and devotion to one's country." I prefer love and devotion to the world over and not just one segment, especially one that causes so much pain and suffering throughout the world.

There are many people who would probably say that I am a coward for opposing killing, but it takes true strength, strength of the mind, to resist taking violent actions, especially those that would only cause damage to the civilian population of the countries which our government invades. As Howard Zinn said, "Even if you grant that the intention is not to kill civilians, if they nevertheless become victims, again and again and again, can that be called an accident? If the deaths of civilians are inevitable in bombing, it may not be deliberate, but it is not an accident, and the bombers cannot be considered innocent. They are committing murder as surely as are the terrorists." There is nothing that anyone could ever do or say that would make me raise a fist to them, even in self-defense. This indeed would appear to be cowardly, but I believe that true pacifism is the only real form of peace. Scaring other people by intimidation or bombs and threats of bombs is no sort of foreign policy that will make us arrive at peace, it can only drive us further away.

If we peace-loving people really wish to have peace then we must realize that there is only one way to achieve it and that's through peace and peace alone. A.J. Muste's words should remain in our minds, "There is no way to peace; peace is the way." If I were to support our troops then I would be supporting someone who is getting paid for killing. It is a shame that our government has to use many people's poverty as a tool for recruitment in what is known as the "Poverty Draft," which targets low-income youth with false promises of money and happiness without hinting at the slightest bit of war and murder. I have sympathy for all soldiers around the world who have been misled into believing they are making the world a better place through murder. This lies within our society and many other societies that have developed with the belief that violence is a solution to our problems. Soldiers are victims of the tyrannical government and flawed society that surrounds them, but I neither support or hate them.

These statements might seem conflicting, but I am a pacifist and support of killing is against my beliefs, even if the killing is considered "just." There are plenty of people, even many in TCAP alone, that might disagree with these thoughts, but we must understand that we all have different beliefs and that we must accept them and not criticize each other for them. The majority of Tri-City Action for Peace are of the Christian faith and most, therefore, may believe in the "Just War" theory, but I'm not a believer in such a theory. Buddhism, along with the words of pacifists of the world, has taught me to love everyone, even if they may appear to be "evil." It is my belief that a person is not necessarily evil, but it is just that they have been influenced by the evils that exist throughout the world. They are like a child covered in mud; beneath all the filth, they are still human, even if little resemblance to one is present.

A Song for Rusty
by D.L. Wignall

The Iraqi man on his back
Mouth agape from whence emerged the
Last reluctant sigh of passing
Parched, cracked earth beneath, but not 'round
This lifeless hero of his land.

How few of these can you recall
From wars long past? Too few, I know.
We cannot name "they" who died for us
Immortal bound in namelessness
The lifeless heroes of their lands.

"Leave no man on the field" of war
Even die to retrieve his corpse
So that, at the very most, we
Can homage his marble record
The lifeless hero of our land.

He was my friend, a gentle man
Gone to war and now at rest in
A stark white forest of perfect
Stones. Gone, but he's not forgotten
A lifeless hero of my land.

The Aftermath:

Continuing the Struggle

Victory?

by Leo R. Lynch

I would dishonor my father's name were I not to raise grave doubts about the much ballyhooed "victory" over Saddam Hussein. This hollow victory has come at too high a price in both American and Iraqi lives. Let's face it: This was not a war of necessity but a war of election, freely chosen and assiduously sold to an American public all too willing to swallow the specious arguments of the Bush administration. Bush and his spokespersons lurched from one weak explanation to another. First it was "regime change," and then it was rooting out the members of al-Qaeda who were working hand in hand with the Iraqi regime. Next it was protecting the US from weapons of mass destruction (presumably to be hurled some six thousand miles with missiles having a range of about 90 miles!) After a pitiable display of failed statesmanship, they finally settled on the flimsy and non-persuasive rationale of "bringing freedom to the Iraqi people."

Let's face it: This disastrous attack on a sovereign nation is in violation of international law. Most of the civilized world, while recognizing the brutality of the Saddam Hussein regime, saw through the thinly veiled motive of this administration; namely, to export American democracy to the Middle East. One needs but do a bit of homework to know that the hawks surrounding Bush–Cheney, Rumsfeld, Wolfowitz, Perle among others–have been hatching this plot for years. All they needed was a president who sees himself chosen by God to execute his own brand of religious fundamentalism, just as fanatical and insane as that of the terrorists whom he loves to excoriate.

This war at root is evil. No amount of papering it over with euphemisms and nationalistic jingoism will conceal this reality. Some day the hypocrisy and arrogance of this administration will come back to haunt them. Unfortunately it will be too late for the brave American and British young men and women who have given their lives in this conflict, not to mention the Iraqi soldiers and the countless men, women and children who have been sacrificed on the altar of "collateral damage."

I pray for our country; I weep for a country which has squandered the good will and the admiration of the rest of the world for its courageous recovery from the attacks of 9/11. It did not have to be so. With vision and diplomatic skill, we could have worked with other countries to rid the world of brutal dictators such as Saddam Hussein. We should have learned long since that violence only begets more violence. When will we ever learn?

President Jeff's Speech
excerpted from *Top of the Heap*
by John F. Bueche

"Thank you, you're welcome, and god bless you my fellow Everywhereicans. I am here to speak to you tonight about the place and time of our current location and moment. Because the final inning has shown its white fangs and the scoreboard has chalked up its nearly final goal. But before we hit the showers, with both guns cocked, let us ... let us as a nation take a moment to consider that which we are washing off.

"We are washing of the stink of a war waged, of a game strongly and decisively played, of a world series final-euphoria, of a match that was in fact won. Yes won and fought and played and done. And now as a consequence, we are washing. We are washing the price of victory right out of our hair and scrubbing the dirty grime from our fingernails. In the service of victory we had to do an awful lot of awful, disgusting things and right now, I'm going to be honest with you, we stink.

"We stink, but not for long. Because we're hitting the showers. We are going to turn that shower on and the water will shower down on us and suds up the soapy lather and we might even scrub with a loofa sponge. Then that water will run down our naked bodies, the filth running with it and that water all filthy and sudsy, its purpose has been served and it begins to swirl down the drain. That's right, and what then do we need care for swirling water, for water swirling down the drain. Let it go.

"Because we know, the very virtues of our standard of living have already determined, that the sewage is not going to land in OUR face. In fact that is the very freedom we were defending. To let the dirt go. Let it be enough when you step out of that steamy shower with nothing but crystal clean drips drip dropping on the bath mat that you feel your muscles tingling as though you've had a good workout. Let us stand face to face right there outside the shower and not be afraid to truly enjoy our gain.

"For you people are the people but more importantly I am your leader. I am a microcosm of the melting pot. There is a little bit of an automobile executive right here in this right earlobe. And right there, there is one of those flag workers from a road construction crew right there in the toe nail on the little toe of my left foot, along with a law enforcement officer and some little kids that work at a fast food restaurant.

"In our society of majority rule and minority right, I, as that microcosm, take it upon myself to exercise my personal majority in making the decisions for this country while being ever careful to accord myself each and every minority right that the minority might deserve. We are a nation of for by the people and I, people, am that people. Of for by you. Be not concerned for all life has to offer. I, your president, will taste it for you and let you know if it is good."

[Top of the Heap *was first produced by Minneapolis' Bedlam Theatre in 2002. The play takes place in the land of Everywhereica, where a little girl with a big garden takes over as president and finds new uses for the manure of big politics.*]

Fireworks in My Rearview Mirror
by Martin Shackelford

Enjoying the freedom allowed by a holiday, I began this Independence Day by sleeping late. Like millions of my fellow citizens, I joined family and friends in an outdoor summer feast. All that was fine, but my celebration of the nation's birth of freedom seemed incomplete.

I knew that in Midland there was a group of people devoted to the principles of democracy and freedom. On this Fourth of July, in their conservative community, they would be asking their fellow citizens to ponder the question: Is patriotism something you buy (with the increased popularity of flag-blazoned merchandise), or is it something you do?

The things you can do, of course, include educating yourself about current issues, voting wisely, supporting public education, encouraging others (of whatever viewpoint) to fearlessly express their opinions, promoting media which allow the expression of a wide range of viewpoints–in other words, being a conscientious citizen of a democratic nation.

Abroad, American troops engaged in another sweep of eastern Afghanistan, still seeking closure in the first of the "terrorist wars."A young American soldier was killed by a sniper in Baghdad–that capitol he and his fellows "liberated" more than two months ago. The day before our celebration of freedom, our President authorized the secret military trials of six unnamed accused terrorists.

I went to Midland, and stood with that principled group, holding signs and passing out flyers to those arriving for the annual fireworks celebration. A middle-aged man muttered, "Get a life," as though free discussion wasn't a part of real life. Some declined to read the flyer, thinking perhaps that they might be somehow tainted by exposure to an alternative viewpoint–an attitude that should worry true patriots.

A young man said he was opposed to communism, as though only communists would question the merchandising of patriotism. Another passerby, seeing my beard, asked if I were related to Fidel Castro. One scanned the flyer and theatrically tore it into small pieces–at least a form of free expression.

Yet most of the celebrants of freedom's day in this conservative town were friendly and curious about what we had to say. In other words, they were the sort of Americans that Jefferson and Lincoln talked about, the sort of people who know the real meanings of freedom.

We ran out of leaflets after an hour or so, and I walked through the gentle night to my car and began the drive home. As I glanced up at my rearview mirror, I saw that the fireworks had begun.

Report from Gaza and Baghdad
by Peter Dougherty & Joni McCoy

[The following is excerpted from reports of Peter and Joni's most recent visit to Palestine as part of the Christian Peace Team which seeks to protect those targeted with oppression by staying in the communities and homes of the victims of this terror. From Palestine, they traveled to Baghdad to meet with victims of US-led terror in Iraq. –Editor]

SUNDAY, NOVEMBER 2, 2003; GAZA

All seven of us got into Gaza! It was a tense few hours at the Erez border on Friday, and finally we got the permission to enter: Noah (Kalamazoo), Mark (St. Louis), Melissa (Canada), Thomas (Sweden), Kristy (Washington State/Oregon – a close friend of Rachel Corrie who was killed in Rafah), Joni (Saginaw), and Peter (Lansing). The letters from the Anglican Bishop of Jerusalem, the Latin Catholic Patriarch of Jerusalem, and Fr. Manuel Musallam, pastor of Holy Family Parish in Gaza City, along with Peter and Joni's grey hair and persuasion, got us in.

The first couple miles in, the taxi driver told of the destruction of all the orange groves on both sides of the road, as well as the homes. A bombed-out, bulldozed area. So tragic, evil, incomprehensible. It was the beginning of experiencing the Gaza story.

We first went to the Alhi Arab Hospital in Gaza City. The administrator and the doctor who is head of surgery told their story. It is so obvious that they have a need to vent, to have someone listen to the unbelievable suffering that they and all the Palestinians live. And we are struck by how wonderful they are. Going through the hospital we saw the recently bombed chapel. A guided missile came through the roof into the sanctuary. Their question: why would they do that with a guided missile?

They are prisoners in their own space. The Israelis have divided the Gaza strip into four sections. Sometimes all military checkpoints are closed, so they can't bring the wounded to the hospital. We heard stories from doctors and other staff of how they were arbitrarily detained for hours, and couldn't get home or to work until the next day, stuck at the checkpoint.

We went to see Fr. Manuel Musallam, pastor of Holy Family Catholic Church and principal of the two Catholic schools. There are only 200 Catholic families in the area. The overwhelming majority in these schools are Muslim children. He is a pastor to all the people. Many have told us that Muslims and Christians in Palestine have always lived together as brothers and sisters.

Fr. Manuel told us many heart-rending stories into the night of the people's suffering, including his own. His family lived in Bir Zeit. They lost their home and land. In great pain and agony, he told us that they are refugees without a land. They would have to pay Israel to go back into their house in Bir Zeit.

His father, 90 now, and his unmarried sister live with him at the parish. None of them could return with the casket to Bir Zeit when their mother died. The coffin had to be transferred to three different vehicles at the multiple Israeli military checkpoints. How it pains him that he couldn't get out of Gaza to bury his own mother!

His sister teaches in the 500-student school on the parish grounds, and takes care of him. His health is not good at age 64. We saw the loving relationship between the two.

We stayed the night in rooms on the parish grounds. The next morning, Saturday November 1, the two of us headed back to the Erez border.

We arrived in Rafah by taxi with Adwan, a commuter student from Rafah working with ISM (International Solidarity Movement) that same day by mid-afternoon. The checkpoint between Gaza City and Rafah was open.

We toured the awesome destruction of the neighborhoods closest to the Egyptian border. We saw the Israeli military sniper towers that hold the community in fear. They never know when they will be shot at walking in the streets, or when the tanks will roll in and blast buildings and people.

Muhamad took us to the spot where on April 11 he witnessed Tom Hurndall being shot in the head while attempting to rescue little children that were under fire. Tom, from the UK, is undergoing reconstructive surgery.[1]

He showed us the place where two weeks ago 65 tanks came into the camp with Apache helicopters overhead and devastated the area. Sixty houses were completely destroyed and 150 were partially destroyed. Buildings still partly standing are riddled with bullet holes. People were killed and many injured. No one lives along that Egyptian border stretch any longer.

ISM was doing home-stays for the night. Peter and Joni joined Noah and Kristy at the home of Abu Ahmed and his family, near the border (of Egypt). They shared food with us. Abu Ahmed spoke at

---

[1]*[After 9 months in a coma, Tom died on Jan. 13, 2004 –Editor.]*

length about their lives and suffering. They are the only family still living on the border side of the street. To the East of their home, all the homes were destroyed by the Israelis. On their West side, all the homes are abandoned. They live in fear every day of their home being the next to be destroyed. Having internationals living overnight with them gives some comfort and some protection.

During the night we heard sporadic gunfire from tanks. We heard the occasional movement of the tanks. We saw the light beam of one behind the house; it was within 50 yards. Apache helicopters flew and hovered overhead at times. Abu said that until three nights ago the shooting was constant all night long.

In the morning, the neighbor Abu Adam graciously gave us a ride on his donkey cart back to the ISM office. It was an interesting ride among the car and bicycle traffic of Rafah!

NOVEMBER 2-4, 2003; GAZA

On Sunday afternoon, we went with Lora Gordon to buy food to share the breaking of the Ramadan fast with a meal in the home of a physician and his wife. Lora is a wonderful young Jewish woman from Pittsburgh who has been in Rafah since March working with the International Solidarity Movement. She has endeared herself to the Palestinian community, evident by the affection shown for her. Lora has learned Arabic and now wears the Palestinian dress and head scarf. She is currently writing a book on the stories of the people in their suffering and their struggle, and their recipes.

We arrived at the apartment for dinner and found a wonderful meal awaiting the three of us. They told how they lived in their large home on the edge of the city that borders Egypt. Because the Israelis have destroyed so many homes there, the family moved into this apartment out of fear. It is only a quarter the size of the home they moved from. They have three beautiful, very young daughters.

On Monday morning we left with Adwan, who works with the ISM and travels to Gaza City for college classes. We continued on to the Erez border with Israel, passing easily through. Then we picked up a taxi for Tel Aviv, to check on our visa requirements to re-enter Jordan, only to find out we did not need to renew it! (Uggggh!)

As we got a taxi to return to Jerusalem, we listened to the Israeli driver's views of the Israeli/Palestinian conflict. He is representative of a large segment of the Israeli society, believing the occupation must continue, but believing that one day a peace accord will happen with the creation of a Palestinian state.

We stayed at the Golden Gate hostel in the old city, and left

Tuesday morning to meet with Gila Svirsky, a founder and leader of the Women In Black in West Jerusalem. Gila, a Jewish woman, was born in New Jersey but has lived in Israel for the last forty years. She is passionate about ending the Israeli occupation of the West Bank and Gaza. A wonderful human being and peacemaker.

She brought us up-to-date on important events in Israel, and sees new signs of hope in them. The signs, in increasing importance are: 1) Ya halon, the chief of staff of the Israeli Army, in the last few days said that the policies of the Sharon administration are self-destructive, inhuman and cruel. It made quite a wave in Israeli society. Sharon publicly chastised him. 2) The Geneva Accords. This is a document hammered out recently by prominent Israeli and Palestinian citizens that presents a total plan for peace down to the minute and final details. A poll shows that forty per cent of Israeli citizens support this accord! Two US officials, (second-tier level), publicly have said that this Geneva Accord is the basis for a true resolution to the conflict. 3) There was a rally in Tel Aviv last Saturday, November 1, with over 100,000 Israelis calling for Israel to "get out of the Territories." This is astounding.

Gila said that two high Israeli officials were led by a Commander to a site of the Occupation and were shocked to see that the Israeli military had destroyed large numbers of Palestinian olive groves. He said that the Israeli government should compensate the Palestinians for this. (Destruction of olive groves is a regular occurrence in the West Bank and Gaza).

Gila also reported that the Israeli army just said it will investigate the shooting of the British peacemaker Tom Hurndall in Rafah that has left him in a coma. (The Israeli government months ago said its investigation into the bulldozer killing of Rachel Corrie in Rafah found that it was "a regretful but accidental death.")

She related that when the Israeli peace activists come under attack by their government and Israeli citizens, many international supporters around the world contact the Israeli media in support of them. Gila said that when Michigan Peace Team is attacked in our media, let her know and they will send letters of support!

We then left Jerusalem for Amman, Jordan, with an easy crossing through Israeli Security. And now, on to Iraq!

NOVEMBER 4, 2003; BAGHDAD

We arranged to leave Amman at 1:15 am for the trip to Baghdad. Arrived just before noon. There is one hour difference (8 hours different from EST). We are at the Al Dor Hotel. There is not a phone accessible. Went to Voices [in the Wilderness]. They have already closed up until

Dec. 21. Met Cathy–wonderful, exceptional, amazing–and Ed. Both from NY. Went with Cathy to CPT [Christian Peace Team]. Met Ann M., LeAnne, a young man named Mark, and saw a Kathleen who was just leaving the house. They are doing the detainees project–making abuses known and advocating for them. We might be able to join them in some way this next week in their work. We see them tomorrow at noon or 1:00 to talk. Phones are a problem. We will email you each day, and somehow work out a phone call a few times. It was suggested by CPT that maybe an MPT [Michigan Peace Team] team might do peace team work in areas where the military does home SWAT- like invasions, to help deter violence. We will talk more about that. And we are meeting people, and will continue to do that all week. No cell phones work around here. Our trip went well–after hearing about the Ali Babas (thieves on the road into Iraq). Joni feels like a character out of a mystery novel, with all this! We are tired; it's near the end of Ramadan fast which ends at 5pm. We'll eat and crash. Will email mañana. Salaam, love, Peter and Joni.

NOVEMBER 6-8; BAGHDAD

We sat in a back room of the Al Dar Hotel. He offered tea, which we accepted. Ahmed (not his real name) is a driver, interpreter, and Ahmed-of-all-trades employed by the hotel. Ahmed had been a university professor. His view seemed different from others we have heard. Life under Saddam Hussein was good, if you stayed away from the government and didn't challenge Saddam's control. Every Iraqi can read and write–not true of the USA, he said. He condemned the US invasions and sanctions. Life has been disrupted for him.

Ahmed is contemptuous of the reporters he has observed in interviews. "Are you Shi'ite or Sunni," they will ask, trying to find conflict where it doesn't exist. Ahmed said that Sunni and Shi'ite and Christians have lived together peacefully for a long time. The West is trying to drive a wedge between groups, but Sunni and Shi'ite Immans tell their people not to believe propaganda intended to set them against each other.

He is very distressed that some Iraqis left during hard times and are now returning to grab leadership roles under the new US reconstruction. He pointed out that a couple people we saw go up for an NPR interview with Dick Gordon are newly elected to a Baghdad regional governing council. He says they know nothing about Iraq today.

He paused, and changed tone. Ahmed stated that he does not feel good about the fact that he is doing nothing against the US occupation. "You feel guilty?" we asked. "Yes, of course," he said. "All Iraqis feel guilty." He told how the Immans urged patience to their people, saying they should wait six months to see how the US presence played out. "And now we have grown lazy, doing nothing."

He invited us into his room in the Al Dar Hotel in Baghdad, where we are also staying. Ali (not his real name) had tea sent up for the three of us, as he continued talking to us about Iraq today. He is an interpreter for the Italian press, lives in Germany and has a wife and two daughters. Ali is originally from Gaza, where he cannot return. It is obvious that this pains him.

Ali says the Iraqis are not doing anything about the occupation. They are sitting back just letting things happen. At least the Palestinians are throwing stones. There seems to be a tone of contempt in his expression.

Sitting on a cement planter on the sidewalk near where we are living, we were planning our day. Out of nowhere a young man grabbed Peter's backpack laying against his foot and made off with it. Both of us jumped up to chase him, calling out to him. He ran to a waiting car, but Joni stopped him from getting in, and Peter blocked the front of the car. The frightened young man pushed Joni to the ground, but she got right up, and he took off running. Peter moved aside as he realized that the driver was not even aware of his presence in front of the car, and he hit the gas peddle. By then a crowd was gathered, obviously wanting to help. As we shouted "he stole our backpack" a couple of the men ran after him. We were so struck by the concern shown by those around us. All of a sudden a young man walked toward us with the backpack! The thief dropped it when the pursuer was upon him. The crowd was apologetic that an Iraqi would do that to us, and assured us that it is not the norm. We kept thanking them, and they replied that this is just what you do– take care of one another.

A friend of the retriever invited us in for tea. His name was "Rudy." He is a tailor who loves Michael Douglas and Michael Jordan. One day he wants to visit America–especially Hollywood. Rudy is glad the US soldiers have come because Saddam was evil. But he doesn't want them to stay too long.

Our trip to the Bazaar was bizarre. We wanted to purchase gifts to take home to family and friends, and to experience this unique place. Our taxi driver, Abu Mohammad, told us to watch out for Ali Babas. This is the common phrase here for thieves. This man is incredible, and probably the norm. He was our driver, our bodyguard, and insisted on carrying our bags. When he parks his taxi, he unplugs wires under the hood, and even pays others to keep an eye on his beat-up vehicle. He guided us through the throngs of people, sensing potential Ali Babas and physically moving us along. Joni took his hand, sensing the danger. We heard Ali Babas likened to the Mafia.

"What a beautiful child," we both exclaimed in the booksellers' marketplace, as mother smiled and father agreed. He spoke to us in English. This man is a Chinese medicine practitioner. Born in Baghdad, he moved to Canada, then returned to Baghdad three years ago. This stately looking grey haired man said that these are exciting times. He loves Baghdad in these troubled times and said life is too short to avoid danger. This is in contrast to hearing that most Iraqis would rather leave Iraq.

Our beloved Mohammed stopped two blocks from the recently bombed Red Cross building, where we stepped into the home of Rick McDowell and Mary Trotochaud. When we encountered each other, we realized we've been with them in the past, running in the same peacemaker circles. They both work here for American Friends Service Committee, doing good humanitarian relief. They have been here since before the war. They emphasized that this is a war zone, changing every day, and that it is very dangerous. Internationals are not protected any more than Iraqis. Rick especially kept warning us. Those not here for some time have no clue of the dangers, and that we should not walk the streets at night. (The Ali Baba got us earlier in the morning!) He said that to place a team in Iraq, Michigan Peace Team would have to have a clearly defined mission and it must be long term.

Five of us crowded into a taxi and drove to the Organization For Human Rights In Iraq, an Iraqi NGO (Non-Governmental Organization). Christian Peacemaker Teams is working to help families track down their loved ones who are detained by the US occupation forces, document human rights abuses, and mobilize a response network to address the illegal detentions and abuses. We observed the CPT members listen to and document an Iraqi mother's story of her missing son. Both of us were struck by the fact that this story of pain is the story of every Iraqi family that suffers the loss of a loved one, whether detained or killed.

NOVEMBER 8-9, 2003; BAGHDAD

She was busy in her office as we conversed with her through the young security guard at St. Raphael Hospital. He spoke with Sister in Arabic, translated in Spanish to Peter, and Peter translated in English to Joni. Sr. Maryanne Pierre, of a French Dominican order, is the hospital Administrative Supervisor, and is proud that the private hospital serves the poor without charge. No one is turned away. The 60-bed hospital is well endowed. During the sanctions they had adequate medicine and equipment. Before the recent US invasion they stocked up on supplies and medicine, and were able to treat many who were wounded. She is also proud of the creation in 1997 of the maternity ward.

Where a portrait of Saddam Hussein once hung, William Shakespeare now looks down upon all in the office of Professor Abdul Sattar Jawad, Chairman of the Department of English, College of Arts, University of Baghdad. He graciously welcomed the two of us. Soon into the conversation he expressed his frustration with the US military forces:

"Before the war we admired the Americans. We breathed a sigh of relief. But the failure to maintain peace has left Iraqi people disappointed. They should have quickly created an Iraqi police force out of the defeated Iraqi army. Instead, they let the gangs loot weapons from open US military camps. US soldiers should understand the culture of a country. Better to shoot a man than put your boot on his neck in humiliation. (We have heard from others that this is done). There is a tribal history here. They dismissed people with a stroke of a pen. No Job. No hope. Iraqi soldiers easy for hire. There is a secret army in Iraq, and they get their salary. Saddam supporters are a minority.

"We study Hemingway, Faulkner and others. Now we are embarrassed (to teach American literature). Now students are disappointed. It is difficult to convince students there is a future for them.

"I now make one-fourth of the salary I received before the US invasion. I used to give my secretary a tip, and now she makes as much as I do. Intellectuals should not be discarded. It is American communism. Also, thousands of teachers are thinking of leaving Iraq, it is so bad. (We sensed that he himself was considering this course). There are no passports.

"The US should set a timetable for leaving. You have to empower the UN. They are the official international body. They must leave a strong Iraqi army to maintain order and peace.

"If you have no future, no peace, there is no hope."

NOVEMBER 9-10, 2003; BAGHDAD

She teaches Linguistics at the University of Baghdad, Department of English, College of Arts. May George is an English speaking Chaldean Catholic, in a nation primarily Muslim. She gave us a tour of her college. She stopped her students in the courtyard, inviting them to share their views with us. Sasha is a strong young Iraqi woman who knows what she is about. She doesn't want to get into politics. She wants a future and a free Iraq. The young man Jameel says he is glad the American soldiers are here.

May took us to the cafeteria for coffee. An art student at the next table asked if he could sketch Pete's face, and we said yes. On leaving, he handed Peter the well-done sketch and we were delighted. Joni said to the artist and his three companions at the table "You are the future of Iraq." They smiled.

May led us to the recently-bombed college library that held many old documents, now lost forever. Then we saw repaired administrative offices, damaged by a previous bombing. Then she took us to the courtyard to see the repair of the gardens. A beautiful sign of hope.

The church of St. Raphael is old, quaint and small. Peter had been invited by Fr. Vincent to be the celebrant of the Sunday 5:00 pm English liturgy. Peter gave a magnificent well-received homily (Joni's comment). On leaving the church many stopped to speak with us. Iris, an Iraqi woman, recently quit her job at the British Embassy out of fear of bombings. She, unlike some others, believes it was right for the US military to dismantle the Iraqi army. She believes they can never be trusted. Sister of the order of Mother Theresa of Calcutta handed out medals of their now "Blessed" Mother Theresa. They invited us to visit their orphanage near the church.

The yellow and white Papal flag flew over the beautiful building. We were warmly greeted by the Apostolic Nuncio, Archbishop Fernando Filoni. An Italian, he is the Vatican ambassador to Iraq. He has been in Iraq for three years. The archbishop is familiar with Christian Peacemaker Teams and Voices in the Wilderness work. He sees things as going better now in Iraq, saying the electricity is up to pre-war levels. Blackouts lasted longer in the past. There is danger that Saddam Hussein could still take back power. All these bombings are being done by his people for that purpose. (We were struck by his certainty of this.) If the US were to leave right now there would be civil war. The situation is difficult, changing every day. He said it is good for us internationals to be here, to be helpful.

NOVEMBER 11, 2003; BAGHDAD

We weren't expecting to find all the children extremely handicapped, as we were led into the Sisters of Mother Theresa orphanage. Sr. Nancy greeted us and took us to the children. Twenty two children, from infancy to perhaps ten years of age, are cared for twenty four hours a day by five Sisters. Only two could speak at all. Some had no arms or legs. All had twisted limbs and little mental capacity. It brought us to tears and tore our hearts. We spoke to them, touched and caressed their faces. A few smiled.

We left with a sense of great respect for the work of these sisters.

She was home, so the two of us finally met her. Amal (not her real name), an artist and teacher, is a strong, assertive woman perhaps in her late thirties. She told of fleeing Iraq to Syria under Saddam Hussein soon before the US war waged earlier this year. She was being watched by CII (the Iraqi CIA under Saddam) and feared for her life, because of her eight-year association with Voices in the Wilderness (a US peace organization opposing the sanctions and US wars in Iraq). Amal returned home after the war.

She shared some of her perceptions: "After the US came, we are disappointed. US soldiers treat people badly. British soldiers are better. American soldiers steal. I overheard one soldier calling home to America, and said he'll be a millionaire. Soldiers come into a house, with orders to search for weapons. They take advantage of that search in order to steal.

"Today, 60% of Iraqis want Saddam back. We have wars and things don't get better. Many US soldiers have killed themselves. They saw that Bush deceived them. More than 100. As Iraqis we feel pity for the soldiers. I talked to some of them. Some were killed on the border of Jordan. They paid Bedouins money to get them to the border, to go home to America."

Rather late at night, tired, we said our goodbyes for now to our CPT friends, to Abu Mohamad our taxi driver and to our other new Iraqi friends at the hotel where we stayed. The next morning, we would be leaving the turbulent Middle East, heading home with much reflection and discerning ahead for MPT.

In Defense of Senator Levin
By Lynne Staples

A letter printed in a local paper last week that lambasted Senator Carl Levin was not only grossly distorted and inaccurate, it was also dangerously unpatriotic, stifling the vigorous and constitutionally appropriate call for dissent in this nation.

This unelected administration has spread false information to the United States' population on all fronts:

1. Tax cuts to "improve" the economy were mis-represented. Jobs were not gained in this country; jobs were shuttled to underdeveloped countries where people earned 1 cent to 10 cents an hour. The United States has more than 6 million unemployed, the wealthiest 1% gained the optimal benefit.

2. September 11th. We now know that much information was known prior to this tragedy: that it would occur from information our intelligence possessed. The warning that previous security adviser Sandy Berger gave Condolezza Rice was that the biggest job this administration would have would be to curb terrorism. Under the previous administration, a heroic aborting of the destruction of the LAX airport plot is now common knowledge. Two literary forms, Tom Clancy's novel *Badge of Honor*, 1995, and the film *The Siege*, starring Denzel Washington, 1998, both explicitly portray US passenger jets being used as WMD's against the United States.

3. The Florida election where 57,000 blacks were disenfranchised from casting their votes with false charges of having committed felonies, some dated 2007.

4. Justification for the Iraq invasion was its alleged possession of WMD's ready to annihilate the world. We now know that Bush's 16 words in the State of the Union address were hyped and inaccurate. Tony Blair faces great opposition in Parliament because of the inaccuracies spread by his government.

5. The "Coalition of the Willing" consisted of the US, British troops, and a few straggling soldiers from Australia and small countries. World opinion was against the Iraq invasion.

6. The secretive neo-conservatives (Paul Wolfowitz, Richard Perle, William Krystol, Richard Cheney, et al.) contrived the Iraq invasion in 1991. When President Clinton was solicited to carry out this plan, he refused. It was implemented by Bush. These same people profit from military and defense spending as they sit on those corporate boards such as the Carlyle Group, Halliburton, Bechtel, Brown & Root, etc.

7. The Patriot Act has sinister and impending ramifications for all the people of the United States. It contains a clause inserted in the dead of night, of which most members of Congress were unaware: the "Sneak and Peak" clause, which allows the government to come into any US citizen's home and search everything within, not informing the citizen of the invasion for 90 days after the B&E.

8. The final imminent danger to us as citizens is the suppression of the facts of the aforementioned information as well as other topics not included in this correspondence. Suppression of dissent against this administration is very well documented.

Senator Levin, I commend your endeavors to alert the American people and I ask that your patriotic work continue. There are other heroes as well: Senators Stabenow and Luger for two, who continue to monitor and alert the US citizenry on these issues and many others which bear watching in this administration.

Statement for 9/11 Memorial
by Mark Kraych

When I was sixteen years old in 1973, my lottery number was 116 and I wondered what I would do if it ever came up. The Vietnam War was burning its horrible memory into my adolescent brain. I was too young for Canada so I knew I could not flee. It wasn't long after that when the draft was discontinued. It was because of the courageous efforts of people I never knew that saved me from serving in an unjust war. I have been speaking out against war ever since.

The cycle of violence that has been waged in our names by our government is unrelenting. It has been going on for countless years so why not just give up? As I stand here before you today almost 730 days since the Twin Towers fell, I want to reassure you that our critics are wrong. We do and have made a huge difference in our city, our country and our world. And we will not stop until the violence ends.

It was back in November 2002, that TCAP was founded at the Jeannine Coallier Catholic Worker House. Little did they know what a difference they would make when they got arrested on December 21st at Fashion Square Mall for having the nerve to protest the buying of war toys for Christmas.

Through a bitterly cold winter, TCAP kept up the pressure. My wife and I joined the group in January after the rally at Bouchard Park. Over 150 had rallied against the war plans of our government. It was the biggest rally in Saginaw since Vietnam.

The following week we set up regular street corner vigils for peace throughout the city. They continued for months.

We sent Valentines of Peace to Washington DC in February.

The women showed us how to get the job done when their March Peace Rally drew over 120 people to the Castle Museum in Saginaw.

In March the Saginaw City Council passed a resolution in opposition to war with Iraq. I want to ask you ... have we made a difference? You bet we have!

After the war broke out we stood our ground at the County Courthouse for three weeks straight. Enduring cold, rain and insults from pro-war protesters across the street, we continued to speak out.

From the teach-ins at SVSU to the Cinco de Mayo parade. From Bishop Tom Gumbleton to the Dominican Sisters. From the World Without Violence Family Festival to the Federal Courthouse in Bay City we have shaped, and continue to shape, the lives of those around us.

The Women in Black meet at the Saginaw County Courthouse at noon the second Monday of every month. The Jeannine House continues to vigil Tuesdays at Genesee and Michigan. They will continue until the cycle of violence is broken. I urge you to join them.

It's been 730 days since the Twin Towers fell and we are here tonight in solidarity with the 9-11 Families for Peaceful Tomorrows. We must insist that the troops come home. NOW!!! We must demand justice in Palestine! We must demand that our tax dollars are used for peace and not for war.

Just like those who dared to speak out against Vietnam we must continue to question the direction of our government until children are no longer dying. We cannot afford to rest until the job is done.

Statement Given in Federal Court
by Rosalie G. Riegle

I would like to speak briefly on why my resistance to the military has moved from protest to non-violent civil disobedience. I am a sixty-seven year-old retired teacher, now living in Illinois but maintaining close ties to two Catholic Worker communities in Saginaw, Michigan. Most importantly to my presence here today, I have six young grandchildren.

They deserve a better America–and a better world–than the one we're giving them with our current war policies of coercion, nuclear threat, and widespread abuse of power. It is for them, for the college students whom I've taught over the years, and for the homeless people who deserve a better chance at life than our miserly social policies give them, that I prayed with my feet by crossing an imaginary line at Offut Air Force Base, kneeling with my fellow pacifists, and saying the Lord's Prayer. By this simple act of resistance, I continued a policy of saying, "not in my name ..."

I have been a non-violent activist for peace since the 1960's because I am convinced that violence will end the world, not save it. Our country had the world's sympathies after 9-11, a support we have largely lost because of our bull-headed insistence that might makes right. Instead of using our power to mitigate the many economic and political problems in the world, we have used it to spawn only more misery.

As Gandhi said, "An eye for an eye makes the whole world blind." We are indeed blind today, with millions going into the military while our cities deteriorate and our family farms suffer. Offut AFB, as a nuclear command post, is symbolic of that wasteful expenditure. I am so shamed and disgusted by the actions of our government in the last two years, especially the brutality and imperialism we have shown in Iraq, that on March 14, 2004, I was moved to do more than protest legally.

There *has* to be a better way to preserve our country for our grandchildren! Please join in searching for the ways and in acting on them with your whole life. Peace and justice will come to the world only when individuals act for it, individually and collectively, inside the justice institutions and outside of them, in prisons and in Catholic Worker houses, in universities and in the streets. The system will be changed by millions of individual actions–one added to one. As Martin Luther King wrote: "Justice at its best is love correcting everything that stands against love." I believe there are few things in this world which stand against love more harshly than war. Let us all work non-violently together for Christ's peace. Thank you.

Statement to the Board of Education
by Margaret Schiesswohl

When I read in the *Saginaw News* that the school board was considering allowing the Junior ROTC program into our high schools, I felt compelled to speak up, to make my feelings known on this subject.

The military would have us believe that this program prepares our children for the job market. I disagree. The only job this program prepares our children for is the job of war. The military would have us believe that this program teaches young people responsibility and leadership skills. I disagree. The JROTC teaches the very opposite of these things. As a military entity, it discourages the free-thinking and personal autonomy that are essential for developing leadership and adult responsibility. What it does teach students is to obey orders unquestioningly, to fire guns, to use violence as a way of resolving conflict. What it teaches our children is war.

In a world engulfed in violent tragedy and chaos, it is tempting to put faith in a system that appears to promise order. But do not give up on our children. Do not sell them short. Do not sell them out. Do not betray your responsibility to their humanity by delivering them to the hands of the military. Resist the ethic of violence that would mistake tyranny for leadership, confuse obedience with responsibility, and settle for fearful submission as a substitute for true peace.

To quote the Reverend Martin Luther King, "Non-violence is a way of life for courageous people."

Let's continue to strive for schools that are a haven from the violence that bombards our children from all directions. Let's refuse to teach our children the rules of war and how to "win the game." Let's have the strength and courage to teach them a different game. Together, as a community, we can commit ourselves to creating an atmosphere of non-violence. We can provide them with the tools for making the world a better place, giving them healthy outlets for their abundant creativity and emotional energy. We can develop a curriculum that focuses on social justice and non-violent conflict resolution. We can create an environment where tomorrow's leaders can grow strong, nurtured by a spirit of justice, diversity, and compassion. As a mother of a young child , I ask you to turn the JROTC away from our door.

[*As of going to press with this book, the Board of Education has tabled this issue. TCAP continues to monitor the JROTC's attempts to recruit our children. –Editor.*]

In the Forest
by Patricia McNair

The voice of the Lord makes the
    oaks to whirl,
and strips the forests bare,
and in his temple all cry,
    "Glory!"
          Psalm 29, verse 9

Through the forest of oaks and maples,
of hickory and walnut, comes a voice,
so strong a voice the oaks whirl
and leaves rush off the trees,
nuts rattle to the earth,
a rabbit quivers under a pile of brush.

The Lord speaks . . . . more leaves fly.
"I am here,"
      "Pay attention,"
            "Changes are needed,"
                  "Love one another,"
or only, "Winter is coming."

Perhaps each of us, standing in the forest,
holding coats close around us,
watching the oaks twist and whirl,
will hear a unique message.
Something we need to know,
that may change our direction,
show us a path swept clean by that voice.

Maybe it will be simple:
      "Be grateful."
And, perhaps, in this forest,
we will all cry, "Peace!"